Chapter 1: Friends (Rewritten) 1

[There won't be 3 MC's anymore! They will only be there till real MC gets to the new world!]

~~~~~~

You can see three young men walking down a road with ice cream in their hands.

"Yesterday I watched Overlord again and damn, it always makes me want to slap Ainz for seeing Albedo and Shaltear as his friends' children! I would fu-" Said a 1.74 meters tall 16 years old and slightly fat guy before he got cut off.

"Yeah yeah we know, you are a horny dog. By the way Waly I started playing Skyrim again, you still playin?" I asked a tall and thin guy who has black curly hair and black eyes that wears glasses.

I am 17 years old and 1.79 tall with gold-brown hair, brown eyes and sharp facial features. While having an athletic body due to some sports I do, I am not that handsome but not bad-looking too. A 7/10 I would say. The two guys that walk with me are Shamile, the slightly fat guy, and Waly the thin dude. Strange names I know. They are my best friends and I know them since Elementary school. All three of us are weebs and love gaming. Your typical teen.

"You know I love Skyrim and I will never quit playing. If you need help or something, just ask this god of Skyrim here hahaha!...Eh wait a moment, David look, that bus." Waly says as he points towards a road intersection where you can see a school bus racing down the road without slowing down.

"Shit they are gonna crash! What is the driver doing?!" Shamile shouted

BOOM

The schoolbus crashed into two other cars and there was an explosion. The bus and the cars are on fire. We halted our steps. All of us had shocked expressions and didn't move till I realized that this is a school bus...'Schoolbus? Shit!'

"Yo! come on there are kids in the bus!" I said as I sprinted to the bus.

"Are you fuckin crazy?! Stop! the firefighters are surely on their way here! David!" Waly shouted as he ran after me to stop me.

"That's no fucking Anime!" Shamile ran after us too.

But I didn't stop. I know that this is very dangerous and I could die. But these kids also have their whole life to live. And the firefighters may come too late.

I reached the bus but the flames blocked my way. Shamile and Waly reached me and we looked at each other.

"Give me your jackets." I said while I held out my hand to them. We looked each other in the eyes and nodded. They know that it's dangerous but they want to help the children too. After giving me their jackets I wear them to protect myself from the flames, even if just a little, and stare at the bus door that is already half broken down.

"Arhhhhh!" I scream and run through the flames. It hurts. It burns my face but because of the adrenalin, I don't feel it too much. After reaching the door I kick it as strong as I can but the door didn't break open. "Shit!" I kick again and again and after the fourth kick the door broke down and I rushed in only to see the dead driver on the ground in front of me. I nearly puked but held back and looked at the kids and shouted "Come over here fast!". But only two of them stood up and ran to him crying while the others were too shocked to respond. "Fuck! Shamile! Waly! Take the kids!" My friends ran over and took one child each. "Take them out here and come back!" They ran and brought them out.

After they came back I took the other kids and gave them to Shamile and Waly who had fear on their faces. It all happened very fast. To carry the little kids around was very hard, and the scorching heat and lacking air in my lungs didn't help.

After all the kids were outside, you could see the most had small wounds but some had shattered glass stuck in their bodies. It was a gruesome sight.

"W-where's David? He said t-this were the last k-kids." Shamile asked Waly with fear in his voice. Waly's eyes went wide before he sprinted back to the bus and Shamile knowing why, followed him.

"Guys! Help! Get me out here!" David's screaming could be heard now and his friends jumped through the flames for their friend that needs their help now. They entered the bus and saw David with his leg stuck under something.

"*cough cough* Hey help me!" I shouted with panic in my voice. The fire became stronger and stronger and you could hear the sirens of the fire truck nearing. Without saying anything Shamile and Waly went to lift the thing off his leg but it was made out of metal and very hot so they burned their hands. "Arghhh!" although their skin was burning and they felt great pain none of them let go and tried to lift it to help their friend. "Arghhh! It is too heavy! Let go! Get out of here!" I shouted but they didn't let go and tears started falling. "COME ON STUPID SHIT!Huoooo!" Shamile's eyes began to wet from tears. "Don't give uuuuup!" Waly is thin and isn't capable of lifting heavy weights but he will try,

for his friend...

BOOOM

~

"No!" I woke up as if having a bad dream. It was clear what happened.

I died.

My friends died.

"It's my fault, shit! I hope you two go to heaven and forgive me!" I shouted in the seemingly endless black void I am in.

"We are going nowhere it seems." Said a voice from behind.

"Huh? Who are you? Wait, SHAMILE! What are you doing here?" I asked the obvious.

"*sigh* Bro we died together, you already forgot? Anyway, I am here for what feels like days and then I heard your shouting. We should go look for Waly. Oh and you don't have to feel guilty about our deaths, it isn't your fault and I think Waly would say the same." He smiles and goes forward to look for our friend.

"I am glad. By the way, do you have an idea about where we are? I thought we would be judged by God and then go to heaven or hell but it seems like there is no God around here." I asked. Shamile looked me in the eyes and then a large grin formed on his face.

"Doesn't this situation sound familiar to you? Hm? Yes! It's just like in the novels we read! Died? Check! Black Void? Check! The only thing that is missing is a higher being that grants us wishes hahaha!" He started dancing and humming while I looked at him like he's an Idiot.

"*sigh* Let's just go look for Waly," I said

~

"Damn, where is this idiot? I am sure we are running around here for some days or maybe not, how could I know. Ahh, it is frustrating! No sexy goddess and Waly is still missing. How long do we have to wait?*sigh*" Shamile said annoyed. It's like he said. We were walking in this void for so long but all there is, is darkness. I think I would have gone insane some time ago if it wasn't for Shamile here by my side. I hope Waly is ok. Or maybe he already got reincarnated or went to heaven? We won't know till we find him.

"Let's just keep walki-" I was interrupted by a bright flash of light that would have blinded me if I didn't look away in Time.

"Ahhhh my eyes! My eyes!" seems like he didn't react fast enough heh.

"Oh wait it doesn't hurt and I'm not blind haaaa~ and I thought for a moment I will never see boob-" As he kept talking I was looking dumbfounded in the direction where the light came from. There he is. Drinking tea and chatting happily with a light ball? Dafuq.

"Dafuq." Seems like I am not the only one. We were searching for him for the whole time walking around in darkness and here he is sitting by a table and drinking tea, that fucker.

"Oh, guys! What took you so long? Hahaha! Do you want some tea? Hm?" Waly grinned at us while we walked over to him.

"We were searching you the whole time and you have a tea party with a light ball here, wait, could it be that you are the higher being that will grant our wishes and reincarnate us?" Shamile asked excitingly and Waly formed a grin while I just sighed 'He took dying very easy it seems, good for him'.

You are right mortal soul. I will grant you wishes that depend on your karma. You are lucky. Through that rescue action, you did back on your earth every one of you got enough good karma to reincarnate with two wishes

"YEAH! I knew it! It's just like in the novels haha! I am so happy!" He started dancing again.

While ignoring him dancing around like the others Waly said "While you were searching me I was asking him if we could reincarnate or transmigrate in fictional worlds and well, he said yes!" A smirk came to my face and Shamile just kept dancing as if he already knew the answer. Well he probably really did. "But the problem is if we want to be all reincarnated in the same world one of us needs to use a wish for it."

*Stop stop stop. If you explain everything to them then why am I here? All of you will be asked about your wishes at the same time but *snap* in different places so you can't hear each other's wishes." As he was midway in his speech he snapped and the other two got teleported? away. How did he even snap, he is literally a ball of light?

So now let's come to the rules

I gulped.

You will have two wishes, the first will be used to chose a power you made that isn't overpowered or god-like. For something overpowered you would need much more good karma. So for your second wish, it could be anything that is not directly related to power. Like money, looks, etc.

"What do you mean by power I made?" I asked.

Something like a videogame character you made I suppose.

"Ah okay...Hmmm, what about the world I want to go, do I need to use a wish for that?" I asked to be sure.

No. Any more questions? If not then state your wishes

"No questions. Hmmm, for the first wish I want to have the powers of the Dovahkiin from Skyrim and for my second..." I went into deep thought 'Would Shamile or Waly wish to go to the same world? If not then I have to. I hope this wish is not wasted.'

"for my second wish, I want to be with my friends in the new world."

...

Wait a moment, I have to ask someone for that one.

"Ehhhh, ok?"

Then he suddenly vanished and before I could even react he was back again.

Good. Then now you have to vote to which world you want to go. As he said that a blue semi-transparent screen appeared before me with our names on it. Below was a casket for me to type in the name of the world I wanted to go.

'I know well where I want to go and Shamile too but Valy...' I began typing in what I wanted and pressed enter.

Ding

[Overlord: 1]

[One Piece: 1]

[Redo of Healer: 1]

"What the hell, SHAMILE YOU HORNY DOG!" Who else than Shamile would choose a world like Redo of healer, well, I mean if you're strong it would be nice nonetheless but to live my whole life in a world like that? No thank you. And what's up with Valy? One Piece? Since when? I was almost 100% sure that he would choose Skyrim. Valy really loves Skyrim. More than I and Shamile together. Don't get me wrong, if you asked me what was the game I invested the most time in I would say Skyrim in an instant, but Waly...takes that to another level. So far that we call him the God of Skyrim. So it was clear what he would chose.

"So what now?" I asked the ball

Vote again

"Okay~"

Ding

[Overlord: 2]

[One Piece:1]

"DAMN BASTARD!" I shouted.

"Now?"

Again

"Arghh, ok."

Ding

[Overlord: 3]

"Yesss!" I am happy he considered us as well.

'Why did I just hear a 'tch!' in my head?'

~Valy:

"Damn fucker, tch!"

~Back to Mc:

*So now that you are all ready you can go *snap*" He said as he snapped again.

Ah and don't worry about morales and such, just have fun.

And I am sorry by the way.

"What? what do you mea-" But before I could finish my question everything went black.

~

So they really can't be together? Asked the light ball.

•|NO, THE BALANCE OF THE WORLD WOULD BREAK, AND THEN WE WOULD HAVE TO KILL THEM AGAIN AND REINCARNATE THEM BEFORE THEY BECOME TOO POWERFUL|• A thunderous voice sounded in the black void, it seemed as if it came from everywhere.

Too powerful? You must be kidding, how can something become too powerful to you? Asked the light ball.

•|YOU KNOW THAT THEIR WISHES ARE GRANTED BY THE INFINITE MULTIVERSE ITSELF AND THAT MEANS THEY CAN BECOME MORE POWERFUL THAN ME, I AM JUST THE OVERSEER|•

And why does the Multiverse grant someone so insignificant so much power?

•|NO MATTER HOW POWERFUL SOMETHING IS, ONCE IT WILL DIE AND BE CONSUMED BY THE MULTIVERSE AGAIN, AND AFTER THAT, THEY WILL BE REINCARNATED AGAIN TO BALANCE THE INFINITE MULTIVERSE ITSELF. THE MULTIVERSE IS NO LIVING BEING, ALSO, IT IS NO GOD, IT IS SOMETHING THAT GIVES US LIFE, BUT TAKES IT AWAY, TO GIVE IT BACK AGAIN. AND IT DOES THAT TO CONTINUE EXISTING, BUT NO MORE QUESTIONS, THE MULTIVERSE GRANTED THEM SOMETHING ELSE INSTEAD OF THEIR WISH TO BE TOGETHER|•

I understand. After that, the light ball vanished and infinite darkness returned to the void.

~

Beeep! Beep! (cars honking)

"Ugh, where am I now?" I looked around and saw that I am currently sitting on a park bench with Shamile and Valy next to me and cars driving past us. Seems like we are in a city park.

I see as Shamile slowly stands up, looks around and then turns to us and...starts to dance again and laughing like a maniac while people now look at him like he's crazy. "Hahaha! Guys! We really got reincarnated! This the best time of my two lifes till now hahaha!"

"Yes, we got reincarnated. I still can not really believe it." Valy added.

"Now, let's go!" I stand up and shout with my arm raised. People will really believe we are crazy but that doesn't matter, because in this new life we will do what we want!

~

✧\(>o<)/✧

~

Chapter 2: New life (Rewritten)

"Now, let's go!" I stand up and shout with my arm raised. People will really believe we are crazy but that doesn't matter, because in this new life we will do what we want!

"Ehh, where to?" Waly asked. Oh shit, since we are not from this world we have no ID's and no money. That means we couldn't stay anywhere and wouldn't have money to buy VR stuff.

Suddenly Waly looked like he came to a realization and took out a wallet from his jeans and looked in. Now that I see it, I have one too. There is an ID, money, bank card, and a piece of paper. On the paper is written something, I assume an address.

"Yo, do you have an address too?" I asked. Maybe that's our house address? Wait, I didn't wish for something like that.

"Waly did you wish for this?" I wanted to know.

"Haha yes! I assumed that you would wish for us to be in the same world, after all, you are the second smartest here after me of course, so I wished for a wealthy and comfortable life for all of us! Am I not great?" Waly flexed. He most of the time is a Smartass but this was really intelligent.

"What are you waiting for? Let's go buy some stuff! We need phones, PC's, monitors..." Shamile kept talking and listing all the things he wants, but I suggested that we first should find our new home and possibly buy all the items online because when I looked around I couldn't recognize anything here but what I am sure about is that we are somewhere in Japan because it just looks like in the Anime and YouTube videos I saw back then. Everywhere are some kanji or something and big buildings that look really futuristic, there are Billboards everywhere too. Also it seems we are enclosed in some giaaaaant glass. The whole city is it seems like. I remember this world to be very dirty und unhealthy...

But here is the next problem.

None of us can speak japanese except some words like, you know, the basics.

"Uhm, sir? Could you please tell your friend to calm down, my child got scared because of him screaming." A small cute woman with brown hair said to me from behind.

Wait. How can I understand her? I am sure she said everything in japanese but it somehow got translated in my mind to english. Wow, that's some cool ability.

"Ehem, yes I am sorry for his behavior he just got really excited about something. I will tell him to stop immediately." After I said that with an apologetic smile I turned to Waly and nodded to him and he returned the nod with a nod of his own. He then walked over to Shamile and gave him a good smack on the back of his head and said "Behave. You are scaring children."

"Ehm okay, anyway I am glad you understand me because you three don't really look japanese." The women said.

'Hm, I could ask her some things about here.' I thought.

We are basically lost. We can't even use phones because we got none, so the only way to find our residence is to ask around.

"Ye, we just moved here recently and went to look around the town, but we kinda got lost so, do you know where this address is? That would be certainly helpful." I said while showing her the address that is written on the piece of paper.

"Let me see...Oh, I know where this is, and I live nearby too so I could bring you there." The women said as she picked up her child and put it in the stroller. She is friendly.

I smiled and said "Thank you! I just go get my friends and then you can lead us there. Ah by the way, names David."

"Hinata." She said with a small bow.

~

After getting Shamile and Waly she guided us to our new home and I have to say that I got really excited when I saw a three-story high, white house with a nice front yard and even a pool.

So after thanking Hinata and saying our goodbyes we stormed in and spread out to see how it looks from the inside.

"Wow, looks expensive" Shamile said.

"It probably is so don't break it. But if I think about it you can break anything you want but you will have to clean it, we are rich now." Waly said in his usual smart-ass tone.

I found a computer in one of the rooms and turned it on.

"Yo boys come here, I found a computer!" I shouted and they came.

"Oooh nice! Now we can get all our equipment online! Let me first!" Shamile said as he pushed me away and sat down.

~

A hour later you can see us chillin on the couch while watching tv. After Shamile ordered all the things he wanted, like new super computer, VR-set, the newest model of the most popular phone brand here, some stuff for his own room like lights, me and Waly ordered mostly the same items.

We had to make appointments online for our neural port implant too. Shamile even got hyped about that while Waly just smart-assed about it like always. How the fuck can they be so natural about it? Honestly, I don't want that. It's just disgusting to make some hole in your head just to stick some cable in it. But sadly I have to.

Anyway, our stuff would get delivered by the end of the week. We payed some hefty amount more for it to be directly installed by them. So for the week I thought that I could inform me a little about this world and then heed out to properly look around the town.

'Let's start with research first'

~

Chapter 3: Sum ice cream~ (Rewritten)

'Let's start with research first.' I got up from the couch and made my way to the room with the computer inside but before, I quickly got some snacks and a can of cola. I believe it's a cola because it's red but honestly, I don't know what this is.

After sitting down on the chair and turning on the computer I first searched up the year we are in right now and the result was that we came here one year before the start of Yggdrasil and that beta testers can already sign up. But because most of the people thought it will be an MMORPG like so many others out there, just a few signed up for the Beta. The company that is going to make the game Yggdrasil was just recently founded and isn't widely known but that will change with Yggdrasil.

After an hour of research, I got Shamile and Valy to sign up for the Beta as well and then went out to explore the city.

As I was walking down the street I saw a cafe that looks very elegant. Is probably something for rich people. Still weird considering we live in some shitty world. I guess it's one of the perks of being rich.

"Let's have a coffee then." I muttered and went over without thinking about how basic or better said poorly dressed he was. He is wearing a plain black T-shirt with normal blue jeans and some black sneakers. All of it was something you would find in some second-hand shop and not something you would wear when you go to a cafe like this.

What poor David didn't know was that this is the most popular cafe in this town and is rated with 5 stars on Google.

Ding

As he entered a good-looking young woman in a maid outfit came to receive him with a smile. But after she looked at my clothes and not-so-well combed hair a frown came formed on her face before she quickly recovered her smile and said "This way, m...m-master."

'Wow, she's really bad at hiding her disdain. But why would she be like that? Hm, doesn't matter I will have enough maids that will serve me with their everything in the future. And they would be better looking too.'

So after she led me to a free table and I sat down she gave me the menu and stood there beside my table, waiting for my order.

'What a nice variety of coffee and cakes, I will take...'

"A cappuccino hazelnut with king cream and a house special, that would be all." I said without even thinking about to look at the prices.

She looked at me for a while without saying anything but what she thought would be hilarious to David if he heard her 'Is he stupid? He is clearly a foreigner and has no money based on his clothing and he is ordering the house special? He's probably some servant or else he wouldn't get into "the glass" at all. Even rich kids would have to ask their parents for them to higher their allowance to buy it because of the price. Maybe he didn't see it.'

"Ehem, are you sure you want to buy that master?"

'Huh? Wasn't I clear enough?' I thought.

"Yes.I.want.a.hazelnut.cappuccino.

king.cream.and.house.special." Now she should have understood everything and if not I will recommend her to see a ear doctor. I said everything extra slow.

"Eh? A-ah yes, please wait and I will bring your order once it's done." She gave a small bow and with quick steps went towards what I assume is the kitchen.

"Strange girl. Meh." Shrugging it off I looked out the window and then looked in the cafe again. There are really few people in here and they all looked rich and are well clothed. Most of them averted their eyes after I looked at them and continued eating or drinking. But some of them looked at me like I am some ugly monster.

After waiting for 10 more minutes she came back with a tablet putting down my cappuccino and ice cream I looked at her, waiting for my third dish.

"The house special will take ten more minutes." She said.

"Ok." I started eating my ice-cream first because it looks really good and the taste is otherworldly. Heh, you get it? Bad one? Ok. So after eating my ice and drinking my cappuccino, the house special came and damn that waffle looks delicious. After one bite I felt like I got a mouth orgasm and then devoured it like a beast. And after that, I ordered two more.

~

So after eating my fill I called out to the girl to pay. She came to me and calculated the price. She handed me the bill with shaking hands and I nearly fainted from shock.

'Are you fucking kidding me?!' Sure I expected it to be much, but this, is clearly a rip-off. Even if I am rich with a possibly infinite amount of money I was nearly poor in my last life so it really hurts to see this number just for some food.

But what he didn't notice is the girls scared face as she thought

'Oh no, this look on his face. I knew it. Do I have to call the police now? No, I should get the manager first!'

She turned around and started to walk before I stopped her by saying

"*sigh* Where can I pay?"

She stood still before turning around and came back asking "Y-you can pay?!"

"Eh, yes is there a problem? This place gets stranger by the second." I replied, muttering the last part.

She stood still for a moment before she started blushing. 'Why the fuck is she blushing now, what's wrong with her?'

"Y-yes you can p-pay here master!" She said holding out some device where I put in my bank card and typed in the code that I somehow knew. After I paid I stood up and left while the girl said from behind "Make sure to come again master!"

But I just kept walking while I thought to myself

'Never.'

~

So like this one week went by in a flash. We got out to do some shopping, met and talked with Hinata a few times and watched some Anime from this world, which are all some rip-offs, too. Currently we are sitting on the couch watching just these rip-offs.

"Ey, you know what. This whole situation we are in kinda reminds me of this one Overlord Fanfic I read some time ago. But I already forgot most of it because the release rate was like one chap a month so I forgot about it and couldn't remember it that well. Meh." I said.

The others just looked at me and shrugged.

"The things should have already been delivered, why do they fucki-"

Shamile said with a groan before he got cut off.

Ding Dong

"Oh, Shamile it probably is the delivery. Go get them in and let them install everything in our rooms." I quickly ordered him.

"But why meee?" He would like to play but not do something like talking to strangers and lead them and so on. He's just too lazy.

"Shut up and do it. Weren't you asking about why they take so long? Now that they are here you can ask them. Now go!" I said. Waly just continued watching Anime.

"*sigh* Ok ok, I'll get them."

~

"So that's it? I could have done it alone too." -Waly

After three hours the technicians finally finished setting everything up. We already had our appointment with the doctor three days ago and now have that neural port thingy. The only thing that needs to be done now is to find a suitable game and download it to start playing.

"Hm, what should I download?"

~

Chapter 4: Virtual Reality (Rewritten) 1

"Go to your rooms and search for some games we can play 'till the Beta of Yggdrasil is published," I told the two.

After they left his room he got to work. 'Let's see, we first need some experience in fighting and we have to train our reaction time. Hmmm, some shooter games would be fitting for that. And for our fighting experience...this one.'

I choose two games. The first one is an RPG named [Aria Online] and the second one is [Will to live]. I searched some more and found something like Mortal Kombat in better. Don't misunderstand me, MK is one of my favorites but this one here is just way more advanced.

And after another half an hour I went to check if the others finished searching as well. Yes, they did.

"So let's play that RPG one you found first and then that shooter. They look cool." Shamile said.

"Hm, ok let's go." I said as Valy nodded and everyone went to their room again to download the games and then play.

~

So after an hour of downloading while we watched something on Chillflix, this world's Netflix, we started.

I sat down on my new chair and put on my helmet. But before I lost consciousness...

"LINKU SUTATU!" You could hear that through the whole building.

"*sigh*" Then everything went black.

"Welcome to Aria Online we..." Bla bla bla.

"So I have to make a character now." After the voice finished introduce the game story and the main task to me which is in short version: There are four Kingdoms in a World called Aria, the Human kingdom, the elven kingdom, the demihuman kingdom, and the demon kingdom. Your main task is basically to help the kingdom you join in wars and quests to defeat the others.

After creating my character I look again and satisfied with it I type in a name and press play.

The character I made is a demihuman. A Lizardman to be exact. Well after reading through the description of every other race I concluded that this race would suit me well. By the way, my name is [Alduin]. In my last life, I used this name a lot, so I like it.

~

"So my task is to take out a human camp? And that alone too? Fuckin high-rank quest." You can see a black-scaled lizardman talking to a person that seems to be an npc. After starting this game David was so fascinated that he directly got hooked by the feeling of being in the game, and not just playing it. He and the others played it for two months straight. The only pause was for eating, sleeping, going to the toilet, or shopping. They also really made use of the infinite amount of money they have to get all the items in the shop of the game. And because of their fast leveling, they naturally became a bit famous. They were already in the top 100 in Japan server after only two months, but they decided that today, they would do one last high-rank quest and then play the other games they downloaded.

But now it says you have to do it alone. While I am pretty strong now, for a whole camp of humans I would need some serious planning before attacking.

"Let's just do it." David said.

~

So, after planning for a whole day I am finally ready to massacre them. Currently, I am hiding in some bushes with a clear view of the front guardians. Oh, what equipment I have you might ask. Well, I have, extra chosen for this mission a full black leather armor set which is enchanted with some illusion magic like [silence], a magic that makes every move you do noiselessly. As for my weapon, normally I would swing around a two-handed longsword but for this moment I need a bow. The bow is a black hunter's bow which also has some enchantments on it.

(Look paragraph comment for pictures)

As for the plan, it goes like this: Since I already memorized the routes the guards patrol I will quickly take out the two front guards without alerting the human soldiers in the camp. After I got in I will plant magic firebombs I bought in the shop behind every tent without getting noticed, get into safe distance, detonate the bombs by magic remote detonator and the surviving ones I will take down with the bow till I get noticed and fight with my longsword to the end. A pretty simple plan but I needed a whole day to study the guards and the tents locations, find and enchant my armor, and then go through possible countermeasures when the plan fails.

"Let's get started." I said as I aim at the one guard that just turned around and went to make a round.

I release the arrow and it shoots forward piercing the guards head after which he just falls on the ground dead. Now fast before the other one can turn around I quickly let loose another arrow that again pierced the head of the other guard.

"Ok, first hide the bodies and then plant the bombs." As I said that I rushed silently to the front of the camp and hid the bodies in some bushes. Then I turned around and cautiously made my way to the first tent.

I used a small illusion spell on myself to make me invisible for a minute before getting visible again.

So after placing the first bomb I looked around waiting for the patrol to come and pass by him. After they passed he made a roll and arrived at the next tent.

~

After repeating this process another eleven times I quickly but still stealthy began to move to the exit.

But then you could hear a whistling sound and suddenly an arrow pierced David's shoulder.

"Shit!"

'It must be another player because npc's shouldn't be able to locate me with all the illusions that are active on me. I've to get out of here and detonate the bombs before the soldiers get out of their tents!'

As I rush for the exit without minding if I am alerting the other soldiers nearby I can hear more of these whistling noises and knowing what they mean I make a roll to the side and start running again ignoring the several arrows that pierced the ground at the spot where he was running before he did that roll.

I finally reach the exit and keep running a bit more till I reach the woods before stopping, equipping the detonator, turning around and

BOOM

"Take that fuckers!" As I am happy for the success of the plan I still have to finish the soldiers and maybe even that other player who survived the explosion. I quickly hide in some bushes again and wait a moment before I see some soldiers with a blinking red HP bar above their heads stepping out of the fire. Two died after they stepped out because they all were still burning and the HP bars of those who died were the lowest.

'Now I only have to take them out with the bow and boom, I completed the quest.'

I ready my bow, draw an arrow, and let loose killing one of them. The other four were looking around searching for the one who did it but after finding no one around they just shrug it off.

"I must be imagining things." They said.

'This really reminds me of Skyrim.' I thought.

"The last one...Yess! EZ."

So after killing the other four I was happy that things went smoothly for me but I should just have shut up because right now you can see a burning person coming out of the fire.

"Shit, you're still here! Now I waited in the fire for nothing, great!" The person who said that is the player who shot at me. He has low HP, it's in the orange zone. But why did he wait in the fire? Hmm...

After looking clearer, he has the fire salamander coat equipped. This coat gives your burn resistance. But why didn't he heal himself and instead waited till he believed I was gone? There's one answer that comes to my mind...hehehe

"Ey dude, I didn't mean to shoot at you, ok? It was for a quest but look, how about we don't fight? Everyone keeps his life and items and we just go our ways, hm?"

"Hehehe..."

"W-what?"

"Why should I? It's obvious, that, you, don't, have, any, healing items hehe. And you look like a high-rank player, you should give some good experience points." As I said that I equipped my longsword and dashed at him while a smile emoji was flying above my head.

"W-wait! No!" He took some steps back but knowing that I wouldn't let him go he took out his bow and planned to fight me to the end.

~~~~~

Don't worry there's a second one coming soon.

What do you think about the story till now?

Ah yes, would be nice if you check out my other Fanfic!

Anyway, thank you for reading!

Chapter 5: Beta (Rewritten)

After equipping my longsword I rush at him but then he shoots multiple arrows at me that I dodge swiftly and continue running at him.

"Arrow Rain!" He shouted and fired an arrow in the sky that split up into countless arrows that rained down on me.

"Iron skin!" I activated the skill iron skin that greatly boosts my defense, but I get a bit slower. As the arrows hit me I get a bit damaged but that's no problem.

I begin sprinting towards him with my sword already in swinging position. I reach him and I swing my sword down as he turns around and tries to run away, but my sword is faster.

Ding

[Mission complete. Return to General Tulikar' to get your rewards!]

"*sigh* Finally. Now I take my rewards and then log out." I opened the map and fast travel to the capital of the demihuman kingdom.

~

After getting my rewards and logging out I look after the other two. Getting in the living room I see them both talking.

"Yo, you both completed the quest you took?" I asked.

"Yeah, since we found a quest where we two could do it together it was pretty easy." Waly answered.

"What? Where did you find that quest, I couldn't find any other high-rank one except that one from General Tulikar." Since there are just a limited amount of high-rank quests every month it's pretty hard to find one.

"Well, it was..." As They continued speaking about their quests Shamile stood up and went to his room.

"YEAH! GUYS!" Shamile came running down the stairs as he screamed.

"Dafuq, stop screaming dumbass." Waly said.

"Why are you so loud, what happened?" I asked him.

"The beta for Yggdrasil got released just one hour ago! No time to waste, let's go and play!" He ran up to his room again with a happy expression as I and Waly looked at each other and then went to our rooms with a smile on our faces.

Opening the doors and stepping into my room I switch on my pc and check my mailbox. There it is. The email with a link to a website where I can download the beta version.

click

~

After clicking on the download button and downloading the beta of Yggdrasil I got my helmet and sat down comfortably on my chair. Putting on my helmet and sticking that cable in my neck I close my eyes. As everything went black I waited for some moments and then I opened my eyes and found myself in a black room with some words floating in front of me. These words were the names of the games I downloaded and installed. So after seeing Yggdrasil floating there I mentally "clicked" on it and then the game started.

[Welcome to Yggdrasil!]

[Please create your Avatar]

As I clicked 'create', multiple grey windows opened and in the middle of them was a complete white 3d model of a human body without a face.

"First, the race. There are many good options but what I can remove directly from the list of options is anything 'human' related. Let's see... not Vampire, not werewolf, not skeleton, not a golem, not insectoid..."

As I went on like that, half an hour passed without me deciding on a race.

"Arrrh! It's fucking hard to decide! What should I take? Think harder David!"

After thinking some more about it I finally decided.

"Fuck it. Let's take Demon. Hm? Wait a moment...what the fuck?" The reason I was so flabbergasted is because in my half an hour of searching and breaking my head over what race I should take, I never noticed this one here.

'Do I have a problem with my eyes?'

There it is. Fucking Dragonoid.

Yes, the not playable race in Yggdrasil is right in front of me. Why? I don't know and I don't care. Dragons are the strongest race there is in Yggdrasil.

I immediately clicked on dragonoid.

"I thought this of race is a not playable kind. Well, it looks cool and is also pretty strong. Plus with my Dovahkiin abilities I will get when I enter the new world I will be more than just a supreme being, I will be a literal god there. Ok David, calm down. Arrogance has brought many great and strong to fall. But why is it a playable race now? Hmm, maybe it won't be playable anymore after a future update or only beta players can choose it. Anyway, both mean that I would be one of the few ones who can have this. Now to the character design."

As I pressed the Dragonoid button the complete white figure in the middle transformed into a human with dark-green scales nearly everywhere on its body with two horns that looks like a crown on his head.

"So this is the basic design huh? Hmm, too skinny. I will edit it a bit."

~

So after another half, an hour went by I finally finished my Avatar and was very satisfied with it.

My Avatar has now deep black scales on the right spots, his horns now look cooler, they have golden tips now, and he is more buff. Not bodybuilder buff, but between this swimmer's body shit and bodybuilder, I would say.

If I am honest I never saw any swimmer that really has this so-called 'swimmer's body'. I also gave him golden eyes because it looks badass. His hair is a bit longer than normal but not to his shoulders or something just a bit longer and also deep black. I couldn't change a lot on the tail, it just has some spikes more and also a bit buffer.

The long claws somehow didn't look good for me so I made them a bit shorter, but since my fingers just consist of these claws they looked cool anyway. My teeth, let's just say made them a bit smaller too. Ah, the wings, they looked like normal 'batwings' in big but now they look like real dragon wings. But as I changed the wings I saw that there was a small note that states I need a specific class to use them, if I don't have that class my wings will be just hidden and I can't use them. I don't know where they are hidden, inside my body or do they just appear and disappear? Now in the game it's not important but in the new world it would be a little ugly to grow wings every time I use them. Ok maybe not ugly but definitely less elegant.

Also, this Avatar will be my dragon form. I will look like a human with horns without it. Just like Sebas.

Shaking my head I looked at the message and button right in front of me.

[Are you sure?]

(Yes) / (No)

I pressed Yes and suddenly everything disappeared and another message window appeared.

[▢Congratulations for being the first player that chose the Dragon race. You will be the one and only Dragonoid.▢]

[{Dragonoid} class acquired]

I was happy because if this message is right then no other player than me will have Dragonoid as race.

[Choose your name]

"Hmm, ok. I shall be known as..."

[Alduin]

[Are you sure?]

(Yes) / (No)

"Yes Lord Alduin sounds nice~"

[Welcome, to Yggdrasil.]

~~~~~~~

I rewrote it a bit.

Just so you know, it was my plan from the beginning to make him a dragon. But I first wanted to give him the dragon race in the new world. But after thinking about it, the demon race would be in the way. So I decided to make it like that.

~~~~~~~~~~~~~~~~

Finally to Yggdrasil!

Now the real story begins!

What do you think about his Avatar and race? I know that what I wrote is not 100% correct but come on, it's a Fanfic.

Thank you for reading!

Chapter 6: chaputerrrr fo u (Rewritten) 2

Hi~

Just so you know, I rewrote the last chapter a bit. The only changes I made are that he isn't an Origin Demon now, but a Dragonoid. I changed it because, like I already said, I have some plans about his race and Origin Demon is a bit too much.

Anyway, enjoy the chapter!

~~~~~~~~~~~~~~

Eyy, I rewrote again

~~~~~~~~~~~~~~

After typing in my in-game name and pressing yes, my body changed to that of the character I made and I got teleported to another room again.

'This must be the the waiting area. Hmm, let's see if I can find the other two first.'

Just as I was about to move, another player, a vampire, jumped in front of me.

"Hey dude□□□ That's some awesome Avatar you have there, it looks really cool□." He said.

I think I like him. NoHomo.

"Thank you, you don't look bad too, like some noble vampire□." I answered. He has short silver hair and blood-red eyes. He could be the man version of Shaltear. His IGN is 'Drakmir Blood'. Wow, almost as cool as mine. Mine is cooler, obviously.

"You could see that I am a vampire? I tried really hard to make myself look human-like, because before, I looked really ugly□ What race are you btw?"

"Ehhh, I am a... Dragonoid." I didn't want to give too much information.

"Cool. Anyway, I gotta go now, bye☐" And then he went to another group of players. Probably his friends.

Shrugging I went on my way again and notice that there are only very few heteromorphic avatars running around. The most are humans.

Then I saw a really buff young man with white hair, light blue eyes and... animal ears? standing there and looking around.

'Wow, I knew he likes it big, hehe, I mean the muscles of course.' The young man whom I was looking at is no other than Shamile himself. How I knew it's him? Pretty simple. Just look at that IGN.

[Aimam Shoermel]

He could just have taken his real name. Its exotic level is the same as this shit.

I made my way over to him as I said

"*sigh* Yo, Shoermel☐☐." As he saw me he had to look up to look at my face and IGN. I am about two meters tall after all. At first, he was all smiles before getting a serious expression on his face and bowing.

'Huh? What's wrong?'

"Hey Shamile is everyt-" As I was about to ask if everything's all right he suddenly said

"Lord Alduin!" He then looked up at my face again as I just stopped for a moment. But then he began to laugh like a maniac.

"Are you mocking me? Especially my name?" How dare he...

It's the coolest name there is...for me at least.

"You started first, I knew you were about to mock me because my name reminds you of that one milk brand 'Shörmil'." Shit, he knew it?!

"Ahaha, let's forget that. Where's Valy? I am pretty interested because he never told us how he would name himself in Yggdrasil or better said how he would be called in the new world." As I said that we started to look around again. After five minutes we still couldn't find him.

"Is he still at creating his Avatar? He is taking pretty long." Shamile said.

"Hmm, probably not. He -" As I was about to answer I was interrupted again by someone.

"What's up guys." Some lizardman with dark grey scales and normal light black eyes now stood in front of us.

"Hi□□. What do you need?" Shoermel asked.

"What? It's me dumbass□." He said.

"The f*ck? Valy? Why are you a lizardman you idiot!" Shoermel said to Waly.

"What do you mean by why I am a lizardman? I was one in Skyrim too, and I became a god. So now that I am a lizardman doesn't that mean I can become a god in the new world too?" Waly said as if it's the most obvious thing in the world.

"*Sigh* That's not the point Waly. How are we going to get you in Ainz Ooal Gown guild? But if I think about it again... it's not a big problem. I will get us all three there and if not...we just gonna raid Nazarick, hehe." As I said that a look of realization flashed on Waly's face, I think. I mean, in-game you can't make expressions but this emoji flashed above his head '□'.

Anyways, after that we formed a party of three and now are discussing which world to start first.

"Since there are only two available for now, let's just take a random one, why think so much about it?" Shamile asked.

"This is an important decision, but you wouldn't understand anyway□." Valy added.

"Do you mean I am stupid?" Shamile said.

"Stop it you two! Listen here, I decided! We're going to Helheim. Any questions?" I said to stop the two from bickering all day long. I want to just start playing!

"Yeah, I have one. Why?" Shamile said while raising his arm.

"*sigh*" I massaged the bridge of my nose.

"Because first, the most heteromorphic players are gonna be there in the future so we could just go there now and get familiar with it before others do. And since till now we are one of the only few heteromorphic players, there will be more for us. Second, the Great Tomb of Nazarick is located there." I explained.

Shamile just nodded.

"Now, let's go." I said as I pressed the Helheim button and got teleported away again. Seems like they like to teleport people.

I opened my eyes and looked around. Currently, I am standing in a small camp, in some forest. Beside me are Shoermel and Ulkan. Well Waly's name is

[Ulkan]

Damn...

I tried to persuade him to take another one IRL but he won't listen.

I am gonna call them by their IGN now to get familiar with them.

Ding

[Beta-starter box received!]

[Open now?]

(Yes) / (No)

'Beta-starter box? Hmm, they are probably better than normal starter boxes.' I thought

I press yes as a small brown and gold leather-wrapped chest appears floating in front of me. Before I could do something, it opened and a window appeared.

On this window were several types of weapons to choose from.

"Sword, axe, hammer, staff, spear, dagger, bow...Hmm, what should I take?" I asked myself.

"Didn't you always say that you find spears to be the most badass weapon there is? Why not take it?" Shoermel asked from the side.

"Well yes, they are one of the coolest weapon type but this decision isn't just about how cool a weapon is, it is about what my build will be in the future." I explained to him.

"Ahhh, I understand. So, I think I take something big hehe." Shoermel said as a light flashed in front of him and an axe that was as big as Ulkan dropped in his hands.

"...That's one big of a axe." I said.

"Cool." Shoermel said while swinging it around a bit.

"Now...What should I take? Hm? Yeah, that would fit me. And I already have experience with it." I pressed on the weapon I wanted.

A bright light appeared in front of me too and a longsword fell in my hands.

"Pretty." I said as I looked at it. It is just a basic longsword but it looked cool nonetheless. The cool thing is, in the game the items all have some sort of weight to make it more realistic. And I think it helps extremely for weapons because if you can't even feel that you are swinging a weapon it would be irritating in fights.

Anyways, the window still didn't close and now there were different types of armor to choose from.

While swinging my longsword around and scratching my chin I was in thought again.

"Let's just take this." I took the light armor with some parts of it being heavy armor. But it's just some few parts, the most is light leather armor and the heavy parts are probably some steel.

So now, I think I am ready.

"You ready guys?" I asked them.

"Yeee." Shoermel said. He is wearing full heavy armor with his two-handed great axe.

"I am always ready." Ulkan said arrogantly like always. He instead of heavy like Shoermel went for the light armor and just a normal sword.

"Why not take a shield if one hand is free anyway?" I asked him. I mean, there's an option like this too, I saw it.

"Well, I want to be a dual sword wielder but since you could only choose one sword I will just go like this." He answered.

"Yeah, but what's the sense behind that? You could use the shield 'till you find a second suiting sword for you, that would be wiser." I said. I mean extra protection is never bad.

"First, I don't wanna. And second, I can't go back anyway now, can I?" He said in his Smart ass mode.

'He right, damn it' I thought.

"*sigh* Damn you're annoying. Now, stop talking and follow me." I said as I advanced forward to the forest.

Ulkan looked toward Shoermel who just shrugged and followed me to the forest.

"Blablabla, do this do that, you're not my boss." Ulkan muttered looking at my back and swinging his hands around. But then he just ran after us to not be left behind.

~~~~~~~~~

Thankyouforreading

Chapter 7: Yggdrasil (1/6) (Rewritten) 1

"Yo, Shamile, what race are you exactly? You look like human but since I know you, that can't be true." I asked him.

"Glad you asked! You know first I wanted to be a demon right? But I found an even better one!" He said while swinging his arms around.

"And that race would be? Just say it." Ulkan added from behind.

"I am a ... can someone make this drum roll thingy?" Shoermel asked us.

"..."

"Just say it damn it!" Ulkan shouted.

"Ok ok, calm down. I just wanted to make it more dramatic. I am a Lycanthrope."
He said.

"A what?" Ulkan asked.

"A Werewolf! Cool isn't it?"

They also discussed about what I am but I think they found out pretty quick
because of the black scales and horns.

As the two continue arguing about different topics I look around for any monster
that I could kill for XP. But I can't spot a single one.

'Maybe they are hiding? What monsters even are here in Helheim?'

~

After ten more minutes we finally found some monsters. From all the monsters I
know I hate these the most. Goblins. These little bastards. The reasons I hate
them probably are the films and anime I watched.

But I think it all started with that one anime where the MC lost his whole family to
these little green monsters and now uses everything he has to exterminate every
single one of them.

Anyway, we found a group of three. Perfect. One has a club, another one a rusty
dagger and the third uses a small bow.

Since we don't exactly know how strong they are we have to make a plan. Even if
they are one of the weakest monsters there are, we have to be wary anyways.
Currently we are hiding in some bushes.

"Okay, Shamile will distract them and Waly you rush at the one with the bow. I
will take the one with the dagger out. And Shamile, when Waly and I start the
attack, you kill the one with the club. Everything clear?" I said to them. Very
simple plan.

"Easy." Ulkan said.

"Understand~ But I have a request!" Shoermel shouted.

"Shut up you idiot. We don't know if they can hear us." I said.

"Sorry, hehe."

"What do you want?" I asked him.

"Could you two call me Shoermel from now on?" He asked us.

"*sigh* Fine, if you're happy. Now, go distract them."

"Yes my lord!" He said with a bow, but before I could respond he ran away.

He ran around to the other side of the clearing where the goblins are standing right now.

"Hey~ Look here~ Big soft muscles~ hahahaha!" Shoermel said while flexing his muscles and laughing.

Even the goblins looked cringed out for a moment before the one with the club directly ran at Shamile and the one with the bow took out an arrow and aimed it at Shamile.

"Go!" I signaled to Ulkan as we both sprinted in the direction where the goblins are standing. The one with the dagger was already on his way to slice up Shoermel but after hearing and seeing me and Ulkan he ran straight at me while Ulkan quickly swung down his sword on the goblin with the bow. They seem to be as weak as they look.

A quick glance to Shoermel and I saw how a nearly two-meter tall man brought down a gigantic axe on a creature not any different in height as a seven-year-old human kid.

'Luckily there isn't any blood and they dissolve directly after being killed, if not, that would be a gruesome sight.'

Now looking back at the dagger boi he is already before me.

"Guah!" It said? It jumped on me with its dagger high in the air to stab down at me.

I quickly raise my longsword and counter the attack. With a spin and my sword gripped with both of my hands I behead him swiftly.

'Well, that was easy.' I thought while looking at the particles still flying around.

"Well that was easy." Shoermel said with a grin.

"Hm, let's go look for more. These three didn't even drop anything- wait, Shami- I mean Shoermel, why the fuck is your health bar down to half?"

I asked him to which he scratches his neck and replies

"Well haha, I thought since they're weak anyway I could tank some hits haha, but they hit faster than I thought. So he got some good hits on me before I split him in half hahaha!" He said with a proud laugh at the end.

"*sigh* Let's just find more monsters, but this time, don't do what you did just before. Now, let's go." I said while going in a random direction again. Not so random because I wasn't getting any near to the middle of this forest since there, the strongest enemies are spawning.

~

"Damn that was a nice hunt." Shoermel said.

"Yeah, didn't expect that. We literally got a whole small mountain of these goblin horns." Ulkan added.

"Yeah this forest definitely has a goblin plague. But we leveled up well for the first day of playing." I said while looking into the beautiful sky.

~~~~~~~~~~~~~~~

Thank you for reading □(→ˏ←")□!

Chapter 8: (a bit of side stories) (Rewritten)

Yo~

Just wanted to say that since I don't know the leveling system in Yggdrasil (or in general anything about it) I just gonna do it like I imagine it to be. I only watched the anime and read a little from the web novel. And I also don't know (update: now I know some)the job classes and racial classes, so I will just make them up.

I will still do some research to be at least a bit correct. And maybe use some info I got from other Overlord fics.

Enjoy the chap!

~~~~~~~~~

"*yawn* Hm? Already 2 p.m.?" Sitting up on my bed I stretch till my bones crack and then stand up. Currently, I am wearing a black pajamas and am on my way to the bathroom.

Two years passed since we started playing Yggdrasil and all of us were able to level up to 36. And since the shop opened a year ago we managed to get into the top three. Well, currently I am top 1 player in the world but 50% of it would be thanks to the infinite money and the other 50% would be the skill and time the other two and I put into it.

What I also noticed, sometime after we came here is that we can breathe the air normally without having to wear a mask all the time. That is because of Waly's wish to live here as comfortably as possible. We all have some upgraded bodies that only the super-rich people in this world are able to afford. And Hinata's husband seemed to be one of them too since she didn't need one too.

Speaking of Hinata's husband, well, he left her and their child alone and went to live with another girl he apparently had an affair with. Poor Hinata was depressed and even had thoughts about killing herself but thank god I could talk some sense into her. Now she lives her life and takes care of her daughter as a mother should. The problem is her job isn't paying nearly as much as she needs to live here in safety with her daughter.

Of course I help her out. I have infinite amounts of money.

Thinking about it made me a bit sad for a moment but remembering that I could help her brought a small smile to my face.

I entered the bathroom.

~

After a cold shower and brushing my teeth I went downstairs to eat.

'They still aren't awake. Probably they are gonna sleep till 4 p.m. again. Hm, but yesterday was a hard day so I will let them rest a bit.' I thought. Yesterday, playing Yggdrasil we conquered a very low-level dungeon. Even if it was low level, it still took us four hours to finish it completely.

Arriving downstairs I shook my head and thought about what I should eat today.

'Eggs.' Let's eat some eggs.

~

sizzle

Currently, I am frying eggs in a pan while listening to some radio music and tapping my foot with the beat.

"Hm."

"I need pancakes too." And so I began to make pancakes.

~

"I should have become a cook in my last life." I said with a serious face. I always liked to cook and then even seeing an anime like Food wars really ignited the fire in me. But well, it somehow didn't come true. Sad.

'They are still sleeping, I just go play without them then.' I quickly washed my dishes and ran up the stairs to my room.

"Yeet." I said as I jumped into my king-sized bed. In my last life I never could have imagined how good an expensive bed can be. I mean if I didn't have other things to do I probably would sleep the whole day in it too. Advantages of being rich I guess.

Anyways, I get up from the bed and then turn on the computer. Taking the helmet out of the special container I turn it on as well.

'Hm, should I further train my martial arts or just continue playing Yggdrasil? I mean a small spar against Scorpio- eh, I mean Salamander wouldn't hurt.' As I thought that I put on my helmet and correct my sitting position to be more comfortable.

"Start." I said. It's completely unnecessary to say start since it would only start if I pressed the button on the side of the helmet. But I do it nonetheless. Why? Just because.

So after starting everything turns black again and after a moment, the game menu appears.

'There is it.' I thought as I mentally select the game I want to play.

[Immortals Battle]

Don't say anything. I know.

So after selecting the game, everything went black again.

So after skipping the prologue, I mean this thing where the companies that made the game are shown, you know, I think it's called a prologue. Or something else I don't know.

Anyway, that's not important now. So now in the main menu I chose

[1 vs. 1].

"Sooo, who am I gonna pick this time?" I said as I look at the character list of fighters I can choose one from.

"Johnny Sun." I choose the bald monk. Why? Because ehm... he doesn't have any 'magical' abilities and that means you have to fight with your skill alone. And that's good training. That's all.

"For the opponent, Salamander." Just imagine Reptile with Scorpions skills and powers. He apparently is the best in close-quarter fights.

[Choose your map]

'Hm, the forest."

[Get ready]

After the Salamander made some cringe noise and bared its fangs on me, we both left to the forest.

Everything went black again.

As I opened my eyes I found myself in the forest map.

Standing in front of me, is Salamander.

"I will burn your soul!" Wow. As he said that he summoned flames around him and again, bared his fangs at me.

"May Buddha forgive your sins." As I said that I rose my hand to my chest and made this ☐ hand-sign. Just so you know, I didn't say that. That's the line this monk says every time before a fight. And sometimes he says "I will purge you." and so on, you know what I mean.

Anyway, after our small greeting, the fight started.

[FIGHT!]

'Damn I like this voice, it's so cool.' I thought, not caring about salamander creeping closer while fire swirls in his hand.

"Whooops." I said as I evaded his fire punch by leaning to the left and then let him trip over my right leg.

But before he touched the ground he vanished in a burst of fire and fell from above, trying to axe kick me.

By raising my arms and putting them in an X position, I block the kick and then make a backflip.

Landing perfectly some meters behind my previous position I look at Salamander and he looks at me.

After staring at each other we start running and when we get closer to each other I give him a roundhouse kick that he blocks and then we exchange punches and kicks like wild beasts.

Every single one of them would've been deadly to normal living beings but since we are in a game we can fight as much we want.

Though he already burned my whole body a few times and I punched some more extra holes into him, we still continue but as I see that even the best close quarter fighter in hardcore modus is no problem anymore I feel very satisfied with myself.

'That two years of getting killed in the most brutal ways one can imagine are really not wasted.' yey.

I already started the second round and he's halfway dead now.

'Oh... shit.' I just remembered something. I found this new dungeon in a really hidden place that I wanted to solo. Yes I can solo dungeons, I just have to use strategy... and a lotta cash items. But that's not important right now is that I never ever have seen a dungeon-like that.

It was like open for everyone to see, but only I could for a reason. I first thought it's a bug or something, but it seems like it isn't. I think it has something to do with my Dragonoid race. I mean after creating my Avatar, it literally said I will be the only Dragonoid-player there is (until I delete my account) so it could be that only I as the first and only Dragonoid-player, can see and conquer it.

It's only low-tier, so I should be able to manage that.

'Ahhh. This will take so long again ugh. But at least it's a bit interesting. But, let's end this fight first, like a badass.'

After this thought ended I quickened my attacks for a moment which lead to Salamander not being able to manage to block them all and getting pushed back.

After I went along the normal pace again he directly started for a counterattack, which was exactly what I waited for.

So him being careless I can use my special move now!

Right before he was about to touch me I activated it.

My Monk moved forward in super speed so that everything moved in slow motion and as he was now in front of salamander he used two fingers of his to perforate him. (While rewriting I was thinking about what the fuck is perforating and why did I write it there?)

After what seemed to be over hundreds of precise and super-fast thrusts Salamander now stood in front of me with a giant hole in his stomach.

But that wasn't everything, still in his super-speed, the monk jumped high in the sky as golden light enveloped him and he got in a praying position and closed his eyes.

As he opened them again they were shining with golden light.

He rose his right hand and slowly lowered it again with his palm pointing at the ground.

Suddenly the clouds opened up as a enormous golden hand descended from the sky.

Salamander fell on his knees looking at the gigantic glowing golden hand slowly getting closer and closer to him while I was still floating in the sky looking down at him.

As the hand came to contact with him he got crushed and then slowly turned into dust while an enormous explosion destroyed everything in the vicinity.

[Johnny wins]

said the super cool voice as the camera zoomed to me still floating there in the air.

'Yeah I love this game.' I thought as I quickly logged out from the game and then found myself in the game selection menu.

"Yggdrasil it is." I said as I chose the game and everything went black again.

~

Chapter 9: Yggdrasil (2/6) (Rewritten)

[Welcome back - Alduin] The monotonous female voice said when I opened my eyes.

"I am back yeee." I said to no one standing in the forest of Helheim on the spawn point.

Currently I am wearing a full body heavy armor that kinda looks like the one from Atorias from Dark souls (Cover pic) with an red scarf that looks more like a cape. Some people would say "NO CAPES", but this one looks cool as fuck. Also it has good enchantments.

And on my back you can see my new baby. My Zweihänder.

Its all black and has cool carvings on it. Also, it's op. I think I could fight a level 45-50 player and win, if there were any...

It would be hard, but with this set of mine and maybe the help of cash items, I would win.

It's like I said before, Waly, Shamile and me are currently the three top players. With me on top and Waly second, Shamile comes next.

'Anyway, I should get going.' I thought as I looked around for a moment and picked the direction I have to go to.

'Man, I love this game, everything is so well made and the map is gigantic.' From what I know from my past life, even 13 years later at the end of the game, only 30% or so from whole Yggdrasil was discovered.

As I keep walking I see some ogres and undead running my way, trying to attack me.

"Come here." I don't even take them seriously since none of them is a threat to me.

Even if all of them were to attack me at the same time, I could tank it and then kill them effortlessly.

'Let's end this quickly.' I thought as I took my Zweihänder and rushed at them.

"Guah!" The ogre lifted it's club and tried to smash me but I just evaded and then sliced him in half.

Without even looking at the dying ogre I use a skill to quickly dash at the next one and then the killing continues.

~

'It's here.' I reached my destination.

Right now I am standing before a giant tomb that has beautiful carvings of dragons on its walls.

Moving forward, I entered it and walked around with caution.

[You entered "Tomb of the Dark Hero"]

'Oh, cool.'

After reading the system notification I continued to walk around.

~

'Dafuq?' I thought.

I am walking along this way and going deeper in the tomb for half an hour now and still didn't find even one enemy.

It's strange.

'I've probably already reached this worlds core after going down for so long haha.'

Just as I thought about that I saw an giant gate in front of me.

'Boss room maybe?'

It has some carvings of runes on it and above there is a giant dragon skull.

As I reached the gate I first used some enchantments and items to buff me in case it's a boss room and then slowly opened the gate.

When I pushed the giant doors aside I entered and what I saw was was an enormous hall with all kinds of treasures like gold and gems but what confused me the most was...

'No boss?'

There isn't even a mob.

Just a big ass altar in the middle of it.

I slowly advanced forward with my guard always up till I reached the stairs that lead up to the top pf the altar and what I saw shocked me.

there was a round table in the middle with an extraordinary design and gold liquid inside but what I looked at right now was the at least three meter tall armoured person in front of me with a big greatsword in his hands.

'Oh.'

After a closer look, he's already dead. He just stands behind the table as if he's waiting or protecting the bottle on top of it.

The armor looks very cool and intimidating and the sword just highlights his dangerous look.

'So you must be the dark hero.'

I was very excited and without even looking at the bottle a second time I directly went around the table and touched the corpse.

'What?! Whyyy?'

Why can't I take his armour?! It looks so damn badass!

'Shit! Damn, now I am in a bad mood!' I turned around and was about to search this whole hall in hope to find something good when I remembered the bottle with the golden liquid inside.

I quickly went back and took the bottle in my hands to analyze it.

'If he protected it his whole life long while standing here it has to be something valuable. At least some high tier item please...'

When I took the bottle several notifications appeared before me.

Ding

[You found {Blood drop of the Great Devourer}/ One time use {World Item}]

If you could have an expression in this game then mine would be a "beyond shocked" one.

Firstly the name, Blood drop of the great devourer. The name doesn't just sound cool, it is much more than that!

I only know one great devourer in the whole game of Yggdrasil, and that is the final boss of this game, The Devourer of The Nine Worlds. The strongest being here in Yggdrasil, comparable to a god! It's the Alduin of Yggdrasil to say so.

And then secondly, it's a world item! That enough shows how powerful and valuable this item has to be. As known, world items are tremendously strong.

'Let's see what this baby is exactly.'

[Description:

A drop of blood from the Devourer of the nine worlds, won by an unknown but very powerful dark hero who wounded it in their battle. But after only able to wound it slightly he realized that he doesn't stand a chance against it and retreated but brought this one drop of blood with him, which he guarded until his end.

Basic Information:

/Rank: World Item

/Effects: Unknown

/Kind: One time use item

/Worth: Not sellable

/Volume: One litre

...

Requirements:

/Champion: Be the top player

/Dragon: Posses a dragon-type race

/Level: No level requirement]

'This...this is just perfect hahaha!'

No wonder that only I could see the tomb, you need to be the first ranking player in Yggdrasil to see it!

But the important question right now is...

'Should I use it now?'

~~~~~~~~~~~~~~~~

Chapter 10: Yggdrasil (3/6) (Rewritten)

But the important question right now is...

'Should I use it now?'

Hmmmm...

I thought about all the possibilities while scratching my chin, or better said my helmet.

It could be an enchantment potion, that would last for a period of time, or a unlimited period.

But it could also be something that could give me like a new power or something...

But there's also another possibility...

One of the requirements is to have a dragon-type race, so it could also...

'I hope I am right on this...'

And with that, I used the Item. I opened the bottle which resulted in an enormous shockwave of golden energy being spread.

I lifted the bottle and with one motion drank the entire thing empty, yes, with my helmet on, don't ask me.

Just as I drank it some system notifications popped up.

'Please be what I think it is...'

Ding

[Item: {Blood Drop of the Great Devourer} used]

Ding

[Requirements met:

/Champion: ✓

/Dragon: ✓

/Level: ✓]

Ding

[Super rare racial class: {Devourer} gained]

'...'

'HELL YEAH!!!'

It's a racial class! A super rare one even!

And the best thing is that I gained it early in the game! So I will have enough time to level it up.

'Now let's check what it can and leave hahaha!'

~ (Oh I know it's a annoying move, but you won't know what it can for now hahahaha!)

So after I returned from the tomb I directly went on my way to farm levels for the new racial class.

'You wanna stay alive~ better do what you can, just beat it! beat it!~'

While hacking mobs left and right and moving like a king, I continued to kill my way through whole Helheim.

Until I came across two dudes I definitely know from somewhere.

"Wow, nice moves you got there." One of them said.

The other one just looked between me and his colleague.

I looked at them

[TouchMe]

[Drakmir Blood]

'Is this for real?! Oh my god what do I say, no stop. No fanboying. Kepp cool.' I thought while I tried to keep cool on the outside. It definitely helped that I wear a helmet and my face can't move.

'Damn great, but why are they moving together? Anyway, it doesn't matter, now is the perfect opportunity to befriend Touch Me.'

"Thank you, but hey, aren't you the guy I met when I created my Avatar? You remember? Two years ago, I mean it's been pretty long since then an-" I tried asking awkwardly, who the hell would remember a 'one-minute-meeting' from two years ago, but before I could continue further he cut my speech.

"THE DRAGON DUDE?!" He literally shouted.

"Ah yes, exactly." I responded while scratching my head.

"Wait, that IGN... AREN'T YOU THE FIRST RANK, ALDUIN?!" TouchMe shouted too while pointing at me.

"Uhm yes, that's me too." I said.

"Drakmir you know the Number one?! Why didn't you tell me?!?" TouchMe acted as if he was betrayed.

"Nonono I just met him once after Avatar creation! I swear!" Drakmir defended himself.

And so they continued to argue while I was standing on the sidelines awkwardly and waiting for them to finish.

"Um guys- oh..." Just as I was about to disrupt these two I saw a high level ogre running straight at them, but instead of warning them, I leaned my back on a tree and watched the show.

I wanted to see them fighting and if it would get too dangerous for the two of them, I would take care of this big one, since I could already slaughter these dirty mobs in hordes.

But I think it shouldn't be that hard for them even if they're only average in strength from what I can see.

"Grrr!" The High Ogre was already near them when they finally realized that they're under attack.

"Drakmir!" TouchMe said as he quickly equipped his sword and shield and faced the Ogre.

"Understood!" Drakmir nodded towards him before he vanished in one of the shadows of a tree and came out of one from behind the Ogre with a shortsword in his right and a cool looking dagger in his left.

As the Ogre reached TouchMe it raised it's giant broadsword and swung it down on TouchMe.

At that TouchMe quickly raised his his shield and used a skill.

"Unshakable Will!" When he shouted it he glowed in golden light and received the hit.

"Graah!" The red Ogre grunted.

"Drakmir, now!" TouchMe yelled while still trying to hold on.

Just as Drakmir heard his comrade giving the signal he jumped down from the tree where he had hid when TouchMe was blocking the strike.

"Haaa!" He shot down on the Ogre you could see his whole body glowing in red while his eyes traces of light in the air.

And exactly at that moment, TouchMe threw the ogre's sword back with his shield and dashed at him. The Ogre couldn't react at all.

In the exact moment TouchMe slashed at the abdomen of the Ogre, Drakmir spinned in the air and directly cut of the ugly head of the ogre with his weapons and Touch me bisected it.

After they both checked and split up the loot they came over to me and I also went in their direction.

"Good teamwork you have there." I praised them.

"Thank you!" ×2

"Sooo, do you both already belong to a party? Or is it just you two?" I asked.

"Yep, just us two!" Drakmir said cheerfully.

'Perfect.'

"Soo, how about I join you?" I asked them.

"..."

"..."

"Eh, is that a no?" Nah, they're probably just shocked.

"REALLY?! NO JOKES?!" TouchMe shouted.

'Wow he is pretty different from what I imagined him to be. Maybe that will come with time.' I thought to myself.

"Yes I mean it, and how about two of my friends joining in too? You probably know them."

"Yesss! Who are they?" Drakmir asked.

"Nr.2 Ulkan *sigh*, and Nr.3 Aimam Shoermel." It's even embarrassing to say it.

"Wait, you're not joking, right? Right?!" Drakmir seemed like he would pass out any moment because of excitement.

"Of course, please join us!" TouchMe said and was about to bow as I stopped him, I mean it's completely unnecessary, and continued to talk to them a bit.

And so we played.

A year quickly passed by and we got more members in our party.

We leveled up, fought strong enemies and raided some dungeons.

And after all that...

"Guys, what do you think of finally establishing a clan? I mean we're are enough member's and after one year of playing together I think it's a good idea."

I am currently standing in front of a large table with eight other persons sitting there.

We are in a meeting hall I rented for now.

"I like it." Momonga said.

"Sounds great! Exactly what I was thinking about! " TouchMe added.

"Let's do it, woohooo!" Aimam.

"Do what you want." Ulkan.

"Man Ulkan you're such a moodkiller." Bukubukuchagama.

"What did you just say?" Ulkan asked.

"Stop it you two." I told them.

"Tch." Ulkan as always.

"Okaaayy~ But Onii-chan, how are you gonna name the clan?" She asked me in her loli voice, but she did it on the private voice channel so only I could hear it.

"Chagama..." I said in a low voice.

"Yes?"

"WHAT DID I SAY ABOUT YOUR VOICE AND THE "ONII-CHAN"!?" I yelled.

She always does this, and I feel uncomfortable.

And sometimes cringes me out.

Not that she cringes me out, oh no of course not.

She's actually one of my best friends currently.

She's very sweet and funny.

"Awwww whyyy?" She asked me, not in her loli voice anymore.

"You know why I already explained it countless times." I said while I massaged the bridge of my nose.

"Ehhh, Alduin, are you ok?" Momonga asked when he saw one of his good friends acting strange.

"Ah yes no problem, so where were we?" I asked and acted as if never something happened.

"Um, we were at the name for the clan since the leader is already decided." Momonga said.

"Ah yes, wait, who's the leader?" I asked.

"You of course!" Touch me explained.

"You brought us all toghether, are the strongest, and have superb leading capabilities!" He continued.

Every one sitting by the table nodded their heads.

"You're cool bro." Peroronchino said.

"And a true warrior." Warrior Takemikazushi said.

"Thank you guys! I'll make sure to be a good leader! So now, the name!" I said. I didn't plan to become the leader rather I wanted TouchMe to become it. But if they all want it I don't complain, I just hope it doesn't affect the timeline.

Now...

"The name, hmm, how about..."

~

So That's it for now

Chapter 11: Yggdrasil (4/6) (Rewritten)

"Our name shall be... "

~

After deciding the name we continued playing, farming, raiding, and killing human players. The last one was my favourite. Sadly we couldn't do it too much since we get penalties for it.

As the years passed we gained more and more members while some others left the clan again.

And after some time we finally decided to make our own guild because these human and demi-human players got more and more annoying as the time went by.

Since I liked the name very much I decided to just name the guild Ainz Ooal Gown like in the original. I may or may not change it when we get into the new world.

~

[Nazarick:]

"Yo Pero wat u doin?" I asked while making the waving emote and get next to the sitting Birdman named Peroronchino who seems to be very concentrated even if you can't see it on his face.

"Ah perfect, I was just about to look for you brother hehe. Come sit down here and watch this." Pero said while waving his wings to call me over to him.

When I sat down he directly shoved a system window in my face and after a closer look I saw that it was for npc-creation.

And not to my surprise I saw Shalltear there.

"And and? What do you think of her, it took me like an eternity to make her. Just look at how cute and sexy and elegant she looks at the same time! Isn't it amazing?!" He said enthusiastically.

'She looks just like in the Anime.' I thought to myself while giving her a closer inspektion.

"She looks good, did you already write the flavor text? Let me see..." I said while clicking on the corresponding button.

"That's what I need your help with since we're brothers and I trust you I decided that you could be the best one. I want to make her into a monster, a sex monster mwuhahaha!" He said while laughing out loud like a villian that just told his masterplan.

"Ok, I will help you, but first, change that ugly form of hers to something less, how do I say, ugly? Or disgusting fits too."

"Oh right, totally forgot about that, let's see... hm, that long tongue stays, the teeth and lips more appropriate then her eyes look ugly too... Wait a moment it will take some time."

"ok" I said.

~

"So here we are, she's complete haha! But why did you delete all the fetishes?!" Pero asked me dissatisfied.

"Why do you even ask, you just copy pasted the whole wiki site of fetishes. Did you know that theres a fetish for eating shi-" I explained with an angry voice but then he cut me off.

"Ok ok enough! I understand that now, at least you left the more normal ones in there. But then my second question bro, why did you write 'Absolute loyalty to Nazarick and especially the leader' and 'doesn't dislike dragons'? That's pretty sus bro, you know she's mine?" He said to me with low voice.

"Ahem, well it just adds some spice to her backstory and everyone likes dragons, just think of it as a hobby of hers to like dragons." I said.

"Hmmm, ok, I will share, but only you because you helped me in creating her." He said after a bit of thinking.

"cool" I said.

~

Chapter 12: Yggdrasil (5/6) (Rewritten)

If you are re-reading because of the rewrite then you have to know I removed his npcs because I thought of them and they are mostly unnecessary.

~

With the racial class I got some time ago my strength soared and since the beginning of the game no one ever managed to dethrone me from the first rank in Yggdrasil. I was something like a living legend among the players.

Not only do I have mountains of cash items, I also have the most powerful character in the game. With almost 600 spells and high amount of mana, added with my warrior like high strength and durability, I am almost perfect in every way.

Normally this type of character build would be impossible, but with all the money I have and my racial and job-classes it was possible.

My equipment is also pretty op.

Walking around inside the throne room in Nazarick I enjoyed the view.

Then the giant golden doors opened and Ulkan walked in.

"Yo Al, you said you need my help?" He asked while waving his hand to greet me.

By the way, he is a samurai. With two katanas and some cool looking samurai armor he mostly focused on speed and agility in his character building, but, he was also a superb smith. The best in Nazarick. He obtained a super rare job class for smithing that gave him some op skills.

"I want you to help me in creating my own World Item, or better said, two." I said to him while sitting down the throne.

"World Items? You know that making World Items is impossible?" Ulkan asked me the oblivious.

"Not real World Items, I mean they will be as strong as real ones." I said.

"And you want two? Damn you're greedy, you already have the most World Items compared to all of us. *Sigh*, doesn't matter, what do you want and do you have the materials ready?"

"YES everything ready, all I needed was you, now let's go to your forge already!" I jumped up from the throne and walked away with him.

~

"Here, your crown." Ulkan said as he tossed a majestic and cool looking golden crown at me.

"Hey! That's not just a crown, it's my crown!" I said while equipping it and marveling at my status window. The effects of the crown are so strong!

"Why do you even want a crown?" Ulkan asked.

"Why? Because every king has one, and as the Godking of Nazarick, of course I need one too. And it will serve as the new guild weapon. I mean the staff is cool and stuff, but this crown is definitely stronger."

"Can I borrow it sometimes? I will-" Ulkan asked.

"No."

"ok."

"Just get the materials yourself." I said and walked away, of course if he really wants then I will help him.

Chapter 13: Yggdrasil (6/6) (Rewritten)

"Heads up Mo, at least we four are here." I said to Momonga who was looking down at the table were he, myself, Ulkan and Shoermel were currently sitting.

Yes, after so many years they still have these strange names.

"Yes you are right, you are truly the best friends I have. But still... does this all mean nothing to them? Nazarick, Ainz ooal gown, we build it all with our own hands! And what do they do? They leave one after another as if this all is nothing to them!" He shouted as he hit the table with his fist.

[-0 HP]

"Haha." Shoermel laughed to himself.

"Why are you laughing dumbass! This is a 'deep' moment!" Ulkan whispered to him.

"Dunno." He shrugged.

"sigh, you two." I shook my head.

Somehow, I feel sad too. I made many friends whom I really liked, but I will never get to see or speak to them again.

One of them being Hinata and her cute little daughter Nemu.

Before we got here today we made a big party at our mansion. But after I told them that we will leave soon and never come back, they cried and didn't let go of me telling me and the other two to stay and don't go.

Well, I teared up too. Nemu was basically my daughter, I saw her grow up from a newborn to a cute little girl.

She called me and the others Uncle.

Everytime she came back home from school I welcomed her. When she had bad grades and wanted to hide it from her mother, I signed it instead. On Parents' day I went there with Hinata. I even bake her birthday cakes. I was bad in it but they still ate it with a smile on their faces...

"Al? Alduin! What's up? You've been silent for a while." Momonga said with a worried tone.

"nothing." I silently said. My heart aches when I think of them.

Before I logged in, I transferred a huge sum of money to hinata for the both of them to live comfortably for the rest of their lifes, also I left a letter.

[23:54:32]

Looking at the time I decided to stand up.

"Let's take a walk." After saying that I equipped my crown and walked forward.

"Take the Pleiades with you. For a last walk. " I said as I walked away.

When I left the room the others started talking.

"What's up with him?" Momonga asked the other two since he knew they are the closest to me.

"Dunno." / "Don't care."

"What? I thought you two were his best friends?."

"And?" They both said at the same time. Of course they know why their friend is sad. But they also know that he doesn't need to be consoled right now.

"..." Momonga didn't know what to say.

"Anyways, let's take the pleiades and follow him!" Shoermel said as he went around the table and ordered the pleiades to follow him.

~

Arriving at the throne hall I sat down the throne, my throne. Glancing at my side, I saw Albedo standing there and looking at me.

'Should I?' I hesitated.

'Ahh fuck it.' And so I did it.

I quickly deleted the part where shes described as slut and wrote that she totally in love with me. Oh man I feel bad- not anymore.

Yanderes are nice.

[23:56:12]

Let's look for a last time.

So I opened my status window.

●●●

[Alduin]

[Title:] God, One of The 45 Supreme Beings, Master of Death

[Karma:] -0+

[Racial classes:]

Dragonoid 5 lvl.

Dragon God 5 lvl.

Great Devouring Dragon 5 lvl.

[Job classes:]

Hell's Behemoth 10 lvl.

Sword saint 10 lvl.

Death God 5 lvl.

World Champion 5 lvl.

Armored mage 15 lvl.

Master of death 10 lvl.

Reaper of life 5 lvl.

Death mage 10 lvl.

Devourer 10 lvl.

Elementalist 5 lvl.

[Level:] 15 lvl. in racial c. + 85 lvl. in job c. = 100 lvl.

[Stats:]

Hp: Over the limit

Mp: Over the limit

Phy Atk: Over the limit

Phy Def: Over the limit

Agility: Over the limit

Mag Atk: Over the limit

Mag Def: Over the limit

Resist: 95

Special: Over the limit

●●

"This is really broken. I feel like I cheated." I chuckled.

Then Momonga and the other two arrived.

[23:58:29]

"It's almost there." I said out loud so that Ulkan and Shoermel could hear it.

When they heard me they came to my sides, left and right by the throne.

"So it's about to end huh?" Mo said.

"Yes." I said.

"I will really miss this, I hope I see you three again. It was a great time." He is surely crying right now.

Now I feel bad.

"You are right..."

[23:59:55]

"Goodbye." I waved at him.

[23:59:56]

[23:59:57]

[23:59:58]

[23:59:59]

[00:00:00]

I can feel it. The power. My body is now no longer that of a fragile human.

[00:00:01]

"Now, my friends..." Wow what a majestic voice I have now, I am exited to see the other two.

wait.

Where are they? I look around me.

No.

This can't be true.

"Message!"

Nothing.

And I can't feel their aura.

I can feel many different things now.

Is this a bad joke?

"My beloved... My lord, would you tell this lowly servant of yours what offends your highness. I shall do my best to eradicate it." Albedo said as she directly lowered herself and got on one knee while not daring to look into my eyes that have a slight golden glow to them now.

All the Pleiades are already on their knees while shivering in fear...

Chapter 14: New World (Rewritten) 6

"Albedo, be quiet for a moment." I told her. There's just so much going on in my head right now.

"Eh...of course my lord." She bowed again.

I turned to look at the Pleiades and Sebas still kneeling on the floor not daring to make a sound.

"Listen here my Servants, I know it might be confusing right now, but you have to stay calm, currently, we aren't in Yggdrasil anymore, and the rest I will tell you shortly. But before that..." I thought again for a moment. While the bunch just looked shocked at one another not fully comprehendingbwhat I just said.

"Pleiades, I want you to go out right now and investigate the surroundings. Sebas, Albedo, you two go and summon all the floor guardians except Gargantua and Victim to the sixth floor, I will await them in half an hour, now go and do as I said." I ordered with my new voice while waving my hand.

"Yes mylord!" They all said simultaneously and quickly left the throne hall after bowing once more.

~Outside the throne hall~

"What do you think happened that angered our lord so much?" Lupusregina asked one of her fellow sisters.

"I don't know but that was really scary, he didn't even say anything but I could feel the rage of his, I couldn't help but tremble in front of our lords might." Solution answered as a shiver ran down her spine when thinking of Alduin.

"You all should stop speaking and concentrate on the task our lord has given us. Who knows, maybe we will find out what angered him so much." Sebas Tian cut in.

They all agreed to his statement, maybe they will find the reason for their masters anger.

With that they all continued with their task given upon them.

~

Chapter 15: Still the New World (Rewritten)

As I stepped into the arena, also known as the sixth floor of Nazarick I immediately felt two beings present.

'Must be Aura and Mare.' I thought as I walked further in and stopped in the middle for them to come and greet me.

Suddenly you could see a small figure jumping down from a balcony, doing some flips and landing on its little feet.

Then, the figure started to run towards us in high speed, well not so high for me as I already tried just now that when I concentrate, everything around me goes slow mo while I could move freely. And that's with only physical power. If I added buffs, time might even stop for me.

Anyways, when the figure finally reached me you could see a little dark-elven girl named Aura bow before us.

"I am honored to welcome the mighty supreme being to the sixth floor, Albedo already notified us about the meeting that will be held in 13 minutes and-" Before she could continue I cut in.

"Tell me Aura, where is Mare?" Of course I know where he is, I just can't wait to see him personally haha!

"Oh no! Please excuse us Lord Alduin! I will call him immediately!" she turned around and shouted "Mare! What are you doing?! Don't you see that our Lord honored us with his presence and you dare to make him wait for you?! Come down here now!" Just as she yelled that you could hear a sweet voice answering her.

"C-coming." And with that, Mare jumped down the balcony and after patting himself off of any dust that laid on his skirt, he quickly ran towards me.

Timidly bowing to me he said in a low voice "W-welcome to the s-sixth floor m-my Lord." He quickly looked at his sister who hectically made some hand signs telling him to apologize quick.

"i-i am sorry *sob* for not w-welcoming my lord, *sob* please *sob* punish me accordingly." He said and then looked up to me and I could see tears in the corners of his eyes.

So cute!

Don't misunderstand me, I am 1000% straight, super straight even.

But you can't possibly say he isn't at least one bit cute.

I...

I just want to...

I raised my right hand as Aura looked at me and thought about what I am going to do, and wondered if I plan to do something to Mare.

As Aura saw me raising my hand she flinched and tears began to form in her eyes too, thinking that I would do something bad to her brother and being angry at herself for not bringing him with her to welcome her lord.

Mare just shut his eyes close and decided to just accept the punishment because it was his own fault for letting the great one wait for him.

As my hand slowly descended, Aura looked at the ground, not wanting to see how her brother would suffer.

Pat

Rub rub

"..."

"Wha-what h-happen-ned?" Mare said as he touched the place where I patted him and his face began to heat up as a giant blush formed on his face and it looked like his head was steaming.

"Whaaaat?" Even Aura was confused, but then, confusion quickly turned into jealousy. She wanted to be patted by her god too!

"B-but m-my (Aarghhh it's so annoying to write him stutter!) lord...,you have to punish me s-since I l-let the great you w-wait for an insignificant lower being like m-me, why..." Mare was speaking timidly as tears already formed again.

"You... don't like being patted by me?" I asked, I thought all of Nazarick would die for something like this. Well, I overestimated myself it seems.

"NO, oh, eh uhm s-sorry, I mean, I like it very much, thank you mylord. I will never forget this honor and kindness you showed me." Mare bowed.

"Hm, ok ok, I want to test something before the other guardians arrive..."

Aura just stared dumbfounded at us.

~

And like that, I quickly fought against some high level summon I summoned with the crown, which by the way still needs a name, and annihilated it completely. I didn't even need 10 seconds, even without using magic.

To use my powers and strength feels so normal as using my third limb down ther- as normal as using an arm or something like that.

I can't imagine anymore that I was once a weak puny human, it felt like I never was a human with no powers before and had them since forever. Now that I think about it in this short time I already became more arrogant than I used to be. That's not good I need to tone it down a bit.

Suddenly you could hear clapping and after looking, I saw both of the dark elves clapping enthusiastically as if it was the best show they ever saw.

"You are great Anix-sama!!!" Aura fangirled while swinging her little arms around.

"Yeah! what she said!" Mare followed.

~

So now I am standing on the platform where Ainz stood in the anime and am waiting for the guardians arrival.

Before, I had a quick chat with Sebas and told him to come over to explain our situation to the guardians.

One after another the guardians came into the arena, while also there was a new face here and there

Aura and Shalltear bickering while Aura tries to pacify them but fails.

Demiurge and Cocytus speaking about various topics while Albedo just stands there and looks at me with love in her eyes, crazy love.

Then, Albedo steps forward and bows to me.

"All floor Guardians except, Gargantua and Victim are assembled here before you my lord and await your order." Albedo said while still bowing.

"Good..."

'Then let the show begin...'

~~~

Forget about Valy and Shoermel they won't be mentioned again except maybe in some side story chapters.

Chapter 16: I am back (Rewritten)

Since I gained, no, became this new body and my race changed to that of a Dragon I felt as if I had no restrictions anymore. I didn't understand at first what this feeling of freedom was exactly but then an enlightenment happened and I understood.

With gaining this new godly body of mine I also unlocked something deep inside of me, better said, inside my soul.

It was the soul fragment of Akatosh, the mighty dragon god of time (or so), and also, the powers of the Dovah.

I couldn't wait to use one of the words of power, the Thu'um. And I just knew that I could use a few of them, and I think that is because of how much I knew of every specific word of power in the game that I comprehended it just like that. I don't know every single one from the game, just the few Important ones.

The only question I am asking myself now is about how powerful the Dragon shouts will be in this world and what the limit to one shout will be.

Like in skyrim the limit was 3 words for every shout, but Miraak apparently managed to surpass this limit in the game I think. And why? Because he was in Apocrypha, another world, or dimension, whatever.

I can't remember it clearly but I think the limit has to do with how strong the world itself is to withstand the power of words used in a shout. (AN: I genuinely can't remember, and yes, I am a lazy ass Author)

So the real question is about how many words I can use, or better said, discover and comprehend.

Since I cant just make up new words and add them to a shout I would need some real words from the dragon language, or better said thu'um.

'Damn, Ulkan could be useful for the first time in his life but nooo he just had to disappear like Shoermel. Where the hell are they?'

While grieving over the disappearance of my friends I didn't realize how tense the situation had become in the arena, to be more precise, everyone around him felt dread and it was as if they are only one step away from certain death.

(AN: To be honest I am shit in writing conversations, like I mean when someone of Nazarick speaks to the Mc. I just can't write this overbearing stuff. I mean I like it but I am not capable enough to do it.)

Meanwhile inside my head I thought about how I would beat them up when they came back to me telling me their disappearance was just a prank and they could finally start their new life. But this was just a bit of hope that remained inside of me.

'Just you wait.' I thought about that white light ball which "granted" our wishes with clenched fists when I was brought out of my thoughts.

Looking around I saw that everyone was tense and shivering...and someone was wet.... yeah sometimes a good nose isn't that useful.

'...oh, oops' I tought.

If Alduin could see himself now he would understand why everyone was scared.

~Third person view:

Currently his magic power is leaking and with his ability [Authority] active the situation is even worse for everyone present.

His magic power is shown as a massive golden, with some black mixed in it, raging pillar that compared to Ainz it is almost double its size.

~

Chapter 17: Go (Rewritten)

'Ring, ring, where's my ring?!' At first I started to look around hectically, what scared everyone even more, but then I facepalmed as I remembered that it is in my inventory.

'Here it is.' There was a dark ripple in space as I put my arm into it and pulled a normal looking ring out and put it on my pinkie finger.

Abruptly after that the immense magic power vanished without a trace as if it never existed. But my [Authority] was still active. It has a lot of effects but as long as I don't intend to kill them nothing would happen. Only that they would feel that it is me that is standing in front of them and with that they would naturally or instinctively know they have to bow, also it can mind controll beings when I intend to do it. It's like Demiurge's Mind Control but just more powerful.

Yeah it's pretty powerful ability if you consider it's only a passive one. Sadly I can only use it for about a minute at a time and then have to wait 24 hours.

"I apologize I didn't realize it." I said as I looked through. They looked like they wanted to say something but knowing they would probably refuse my apology saying it's unnecessary I continued.

"So what was it we were talking about?" I asked them.

"My lord, if you would allow me I would explain our situation to the others." Sebas said to me from the side while bowing respectfully I can still see the cold sweat running down his forehead.

"Go ahead." I said. Did I already mention how majestic my new voice is?

~

After Sebas explained everything and I gave the corresponding orders (Just what Ainz said in the anime) I at first wanted to ask what they think about me like Ainz did but then I thought it as unnecessary, instead, I want to test my powers as a Dovahkin. But I don't want to use it in here because I still don't know how powerful it will be.

If it's just like in the game then I don't have to worry but if it's like I once heard from Valy then I should be careful. Waly once told me that the shouts are shown very very weak in comparison of what they could do normally. And he told me that the dragons in Skyrim are also a very watered down version of what they should be normally.

Anyways, let's go do some shouting!

"Listen up." I said, not even loud but the guardians that were talking about our current situation instantly became silent and listened to me.

"I want every Guardian present, and Sebas, to follow me outside of Nazarick, the rest, are to guard Nazarick while we are out." I said and then teleported with the ring of Ainz Ooal Gown to the entrance of Nazarick.

The other Guardians were confused as to why their lord would want to go out so suddenly, especially with their current situation.

They stood up and were about to follow their lord.

Suddenly, Demiurge spoke up. "Hmm."

"What is it, Demiurge?" Albedo asked.

(AN: Short info before I let Demiurge speak his mind. As you know, the beings in Nazarick especially Demiurge and Albedo, have all very high intelligence. And that makes me wonder if I will be able to write about them. I will try my best but if you find any logic error, instead of mocking me for my puny intelligence could you tell me what's wrong so that I could correct it? Would be very nice of you!)

"Thank you for listening to me. Why do you think Alduin-sama wish to take us outside considering our current situation? Shouldn't we prepare for the worst? Like an unknown enemy attacking Nazarick? And shouldn't we send spies outside first? We have no-"

before Demiurge could continue to ask Albedo interrupted.

"DEMIURGE! You dare question our Lord?" Albedo shouted while she pointed a finger at Demiurge who flinched at this movement.

The others also didn't agree with Demiurge.

Meanwhile Albedo went full yandere mode and said "Demiurge I hope you don't plan on defying Lord Alduin-sama's orders." while smiling scarily.

"N-no definitely not, I didn't mean it that way. I just wanted to know what our great lord has planned to know how I can improve in future to please our lords." Demiurge said while bowing.

"Enough." Sebas Tian said. As the situation began to calm down. Demiurge was just like always trying to find out his lords next steps and be useful to him but the others didn't take it that way and thought maybe he dares to defy their lord and that is a major sin to say so.

~Back to Alduin.

As I was waiting at the entrance to Nazarick for the other ones to arrive my patience was running out.

'Why are they taking so long?' I thought.

But just as I thought about it they all appeared on the stairs leading up.

"Follow me." I said and turned around to continue walking.

Suddenly Albedo rushed forward and began walking nearly next to me. Much to the annoyance of Shalltear.

~

Chapter 18: Soft heaven (Rewritten)

Continuing to walk we finally reached outside of Nazarick.

Standing there in all might with black golden armor I thought to myself.

'I should probably take some distance from Nazarick and with some I mean some hundred miles maybe, better safe than sorry.'

I turned around and looked at my subjects.

"You all wait here for a moment, I will open a Gate for you shortly." I said.

"Yes my lord." All of them said in sync while bowing.

I turned around and... Vanished, and then several loud explosions were heard and a giant shockwave blasted against them, but it didn't do more than wave their hair in the wind.

In reality I was running at maximum speed and everything slowed down for me.

Honestly, it feels strange, it's like I am deep underwater and some heavy pressure is formed on me.

Instead of going to where I wanted to at first I got so in the amazing feeling of running around while everyone else is moving extremly slow.

Suddenly I stopped.

"Oooohhh neeaat Iii doonntt neeedd too rruuunn! Whhaaat thee hhheelll?" Okay that is strange.

Seems like my mouth and vocal cords can't keep up.

So I can walk and even stand still in this state? That's nice.

I am pretty unbeatable right now hehe. Being a speedster is op as hell, I don't understand why flash and magnetos boy (forgot his name) in the movies are such losers.

Anyway.

Looking around I saw the guardians still at the spot where I left them before.

I walked up to them and looked.

The guardians are bowing in the direction I was standing before I took off.

"Hmm" Looking left then right I made so one was looking and went to Albedo.

She was bowing forward so I had a great view of her ass. And that white dress she is wearing only made her more alluring.

'What a beautiful ass.' Looking left and right again I gave it a good long light squeeze.

'Ahhh my hand is in heaven right now.'

Squeezing it a bit longer and giving it a VERY light slap I left the soft heaven behind and was ashamed for a second for molestating a girl but just a second as she probably would love to be molested by me.

I just hope her ass is strong enough to not be blasted apart from that slap in superspeed, I did it extra carefully... Oh man now I am regretting it.

'Maybe I should stop fooling around and get going'

Chapter 19: Fus.. Roh...-and you know the rest (Rewritten)

So I ran somewhere quiet with no human settlements in the surrounding, only some small goblin tribes, some trolls and other weak monster around. There are only mountains and a giant grassland around.

I don't want to kill humans so soon as I am still not sure how I will react. And I know I have to kill a lot of humans.

"Go away depressing thoughts!"

'Okay this place is good let's open a gate. You got this Alduin.'

Pointing my arm forward I imagined a portal to form that leads to Momonga and the others.

"Gate."

portal opening noises

"Hi there." A portal opened in front of Albedo as she looked inside warily at first but after she made sure it is really me on the other side she stepped trough it and the others followed, but after she and the others stepped through it they looked at me for a while without saying anything.

I looked to my side and saw Albedo was looking at the ground but as she looked up I saw a very red face and as she saw that I looked at her she started squirming around and made +18 adult noises.

Standing there in my armor I contemplated about what to do now. Hmm now that I think about it, I need a cool robe as well, can't keep running around in armor all the time, even if it looks cool.

If someone would ask they would all agree that today was the most stressing day since they were created. First Nazarick gets taken to another foreign world, then their lord uses extreme pressure on them for a reason they yet have to find out, then order them to follow him outside. Truly, a stressful day for us Guardians.

"Now, my subjects, I know it might be confusing for you. "Why did he take us here? Shouldn't we strengthen Nazaricks defenses and send out troops to gather information first?" As I talked Demiurge felt extreme shame as he thought his Lord was talking about him.

"Of course these questions are justified and I advice everyone of you to think like that, for Nazarick." I continued as Demiurge swore to himself that he will try even more to please his lord.

"But don't worry I have everything under control, I will give you all proper tasks once we get back and I expect all of you to take them seriously and do your best!" It's nice to talk like that.

"Yes Alduin sama!" They all said in sync.

"Now then, let's finally get to the point. I brought you all here to show you something."

After this I turned to the direction of the mountains and concentrated myself.

All of the people present at first were curious about what I want to show them but then felt extrem fear.

"n-n-nee ch-chan uwaa!" Poor Mare.

"This power, truly only my lord would be capable of something like that" Demiurge said while shaking himself.

"Oh. My. Lord. This. Is. The. Power. Of. A. True. Warrior." Cocytus said while being on his knees and it looks like he's crying? No, must be my imagination.

Meanwhile I was having the time of my life.

'I just took a breath and felt something deep inside me, as I reached for it I felt like a true dragon! This power! Now let's get to it!' I thought as I took even more air inside my lungs.

"Fus..."

"Roh..." Oh I can already feel it in my throat.

"DAAA!!!!"

~~~

YOU THOUGHT IT WAS THE REST OF THE CHAPTER BUT IT WAS ME, DIO DAAA

~~~

Oops seems like the chapter ended here.

How did you like it? Hahahahaha! YOU SHALL SUFFER! Until the next chapter.

By the way I didn't want to

~~~

.

.

.

.

.

.

.

Nah I was just joking

Here:

~~~

"DAAA!!!!"

It was quiet for a short moment, but this silence was pain for everyone except myself.

Before suddenly a very very loud explosion occurred and took everyones attention.

They looked at the giant dust cloud in front of their lord.

For a moment it seemed like his back was their entire world, his shadow engulfing them all.

As the dust cloud settled they couldn't believe their eyes and their mouths fell open.

What they saw was a giant paved way. (I don't know how to call it so we will just go with that, just remember that scene where saitama fights Genos and what happened)

The trees probably turned to dust and the mountains were pulverized. And this stretched over a hundred miles and there was no end in sight.

With this, new formed respect was won again as all the guardians kneeled down with head hung low with immense pride that they are allowed to serve such a being but also fear of his power and if they will be good enough for him.

But I was in my own world again.

'This, this is great! So much power I couldn't believe it! Hahahaha!' I thought.

"WE ARE DONE HERE LET US RETURN HOME!" I said to my subjects.

"Gate." I opened a gate again and walked towards it while walking past the kneeling Guardians who also were shivering and walked trough it with a crazy smile on my face that the others couldn't notice because of my helmet.

But instead of following him the guardians continued to kneel until I was through the gate. After that some collapsed on the floor while panting hard and some also had a crazy smile on their faces.

But Albedo had a smile of bliss and craziness on her face and Shalltear was out cold becaue of too much stimulation. While this whole fiasco she came multiple times but after she saw what her lord did and how he ordered them with clear might in his voice she couldn't take it and collapsed while twitching.

"Come on now, let us go home." Albedo said while elegantly walking through the gate with a smile on her face.

Everyone who could walked through the gate following Albedos lead.

While Aura picked up Shalltear from the collar of her dress and walked through the gate while Shalltear continued to mumble some incomprehensible words and moaned from time to time.

~~~~

Okay that's it for real, thank you for reading!

Chapter 20: "That's not what I wished for!" (Rewritten)

"Argh, what the hell? Who the hell used that damn flashbomb spell inside?!" I shouted.

Man, I was so excited, this should be an epic moment of me and my friends entering the new world and beginning our true adventure, but noooo! Someone had to ruin it! I bet it was that big ball of old-man white hair Shoermel trying to make some cool entrance!

I was slowly regaining my sight as I heard screaming and murmurs all around me.

"WHO ARE YOU AND HOW DID YOU GET IN HERE?!" Someone shouted.

'Wait where am I and is this dude talking to me?!' I thought. I was standing in some dark hall while there were some robed people in front of me. Oh I just realized that I am standing on some magic circle.

"Hey hey! Dare to shout at me again and your heads are flying!" I shouted and reached for my swords... Swords? Wait, WHERE ARE MY KATANAS?!

I started looking around hectically as I also realized my armor is missing. And the only thing I am wearing on my toned, red scaled body, is some towel of sorts around my waist. Kinda like skyrim when you run around naked.

'Ahh, they're in my inventory for sure, heh, I'm so smart.' I thought as I stretched out my arm to access my inventory as a dark rift in space appeared and I put my hand inside.

"huhhhhh!!?" My smile slowly faded away and a frown formed on my face.

"Where the heck are we and what are those stupid weapons in our hands, I can't remove mine!?" Some dude screamed at the robed people who were confused about the whole situation.

It seems there are four other persons who just got here and have no clue what's going on, also they all have weapons like one has a Bow, one a sword, one a spear and one a... Shield?

"Wait a damn moment..." I spoke out unconsciously.

"...Why the hell am I in the rising of the shield hero?!" As I said that the three of the four other heros looked at the one with the shield as he seemed to be proud?

"You, Demihuman, could it be that you're t-the fifth h-hero?!" One of the robed people which I think are mages called out while pointing at me.

"No you idiot! He must have been caught in the summoning spell somehow and is probably from another world. Just look at him!" The other mage said to which I suppose is his junior.

"Oi, I would think twice before saying something like that to me if I were you!" I said while giving him my killer glare to which he flinched.

I mean ok I am a Demihuman, but a handsome one at least! Just look at all those fiery red, unbreakable, smooth scales of mine! Plus my shiny white teeth. Also I think I am the most ripped Demihuman they will ever see! (If someone still doesn't understand, it's Ulkans POV)

I can understand if humans don't find me attractive, but I am out for more exotic things anyway hehehe.

Anyway.

'What the hell is even going on here?! *Sigh* I should play along and see what comes out at the end. And if they decide to make me their enemy, I won't hesitate to take that whole Royal family down and take over their lands hehehe, doesn't sound that bad.'

But now comes the real problem. Where are Alduin and Shoermel and why am I in the universe of the raising of the shield hero? Also why are all my goddamn items missing?

As I thought hard about all these questions the other four heros decided to talk with the robed people about what is happening and they told them all about the 'We summoned you and now help us' shit which they apparently had only little to no problems with.

'The only thing I have are my magic, stats and skills. But if I think about it, even with only those, I would just need a good sword and the world could literally do nothing against me hahahaha!' While I was in my thoughts again one of the mages spoke to me.

"Um, you! Demihuman!" What's up with these damn racists!

"Call me Ulkan." I said.

"What a strange name... But doesn't matter, you seem to have been caught in our summoning of the heros but we can't send you back to your world so we give you two choices." He said lifting two fingers.

"Shoot."

"What where?! Who is shooting?" He looked around hectically trying to see if somebody was about to shoot him on my command.

sigh I shook my head.

"Just tell me what choices you are proposing damnit!"

"Hey don't yell at him!" The young one said.

"Shut up milk-drinker!" I said back.

"ok."

"Now tell me what choices you are thinking you could force me to choose from." I said. I am quite intimidating if I say so myself. I am at least two meters tall with sharp golden eyes that seem to have flames dancing inside them.

"Grr, first! You strength will be tested and you could join the heroes in protecting humanity."

"Go on." I said.

The other people in the hall decided to listen too.

"Second, you will be sold off to the slave trader as a rare good hehe." An evil grin made it across his face.

'Bah, almost forgot these ugly humans have slaves here and treat them like shit and worse. But if they think they can do what they want with me they are wrong, very wrong.'

" You can't do that! It wasn't his fault for being caught in your summoning!" Oh how sweet of you Naofumi.

"Hero of the shield, please don't interfere. Come on, I will show you revered Heros your rooms, you should rest for today and tomorrow you will meet the king himself!"

"But-" He wanted to say more but the guy with the spear took him by the shoulder.

"Aww come on shield guy! Aren't you the least interested in how a fantasy worlds castle looks from the inside? Maybe we will find some cute maids too! Forget that lizard guy, I am sure he is smart enough to choose the first option and maybe we will see him again tomorrow, right?" He asked the mage.

"That's right. Now please follow me." The mage said and walked away, while the Heros followed him. Naofumi gave me a last look and followed them.

"Now, Demihu-" He started.

"I said call. Me. Ulkan." I glared at him.

"Now... Ulkan, what do you choose?"

"What do you plan to do if I choose neither of them?" I asked.

"Kill you." He said slowly.

Now it was my time to smile sinister. My sharp teeth showing and dark red aura exploding from me.

"Kill me? Is that so?"

"W-what are y-you doing!?"

"Then..." I took a step forward to which all of them fliched because of the loud cracking noise from the cold stone floor.

"Hiii! Mama!" The young one shouted.

"Then I would choose the first one." I said as the whole aura vanished and everyone realeased their breath.

"Why make it so dramatic..." Is what everyone thought but no one spoke because they now feared me.

"S-so be it, then f-follow me!" He said and started walking down the hall where the heros went too.

As I walked behind him I thought to myself.

'As much I would like to burn down the whole royal family with my demonic fire and take over their kindom, it wouldn't work.'

I mean the killing part would but not the taking over one, at least not that fast and not that way. No human in this world would follow a demihumans order except they have some weird fetish and because of that I will have to play slow for now. Also, I need to find out more about my situation.

Chapter 21: "Cool, but how do I get back?" (Rewritten)

"Aw man, Ulkan, why are you always trying to mess with me huh?" That stupid lizard used a flashbang spell right into my face! It should be a legendary moment but noooo he had to ruin it.

Sniff sniff

"Ewww who the hell shit inside of Nazarick, that's disgusting guys!"

Standing up I realized that I am in some kind of cell?

"Ehhh what the-"

"NOW SHUT THE HELL UP YOU DAMN DOG, ALWAYS TALKING SHIT DAMNIT!" Suddenly some guy in armor came and shouted at me?!

"Heyheyhey, don't do that again, got me?" I said while walking toward the steel bars. I just realized that I am almost naked with only some kind of towel on my private parts.

But I don't care, now everyone can see these muscles, yeah.

Anyway.

The dude on the other side of the bars seemed like he would explode any second but then quickly calmed down again.

I don't like that.

"Haa? Too scared to talk anymore you little shit? Look at you standing behind this thin metal bars and thinking you are safe hahaha!"

Oooh now he's angry again!

"YOU DARE!" He shouted at me but still seemed relucant.

"I do." Hehe.

"Grrr.."

"Hey hey, who's the dog here? Stop growling at me, bah." Oh man that dude is fun!

"If it weren't for the princess ordering us to let you be until she talked to you.... You would wish you never were born. I would-"

"Oooh so scary, anyway, tell me more about that princess you just talked about. I don't even know where I am..."

I just appeared in this shit reeking cell and then got shouted at from some weak ass guard. That's ridiculous! Where the hell are Alduin and Ulkan? Damn I swear if this is a prank... I will beat Ulkan up for sure, and then together we will beat Alduin up!

"What? Bit off your tongue? Talk." Man, should I just walk outta here? I really don't want to talk to some shit anymore while having the stench of shit in my nose all the time.

But on the other hand I want to see that princess... I hope she's a hot busty princess... I really hope that.

I also could just break out and search her... But they would all attack me and even though I could probably deal with anyone here it would still be annoying aaand maybe there's someone stronger than me here so let's play it safe.

"Tch, just you wait, I will make your life the living hell!" He said before walking away.

"Then I will just wait." With a shrug I turned around and wanted to sit down somewhere, but everything was so dirty!

sigh

Then I will just take something from my inventory, I should have that chair I forgot to take out...

Stretching my hand out I clawed at the space before me which produced black ripped portal where I put my hand inside.

"WHAT?!" I screamed. My scream was so loud that even the people outside of the underground prison could hear it.

And in the cell next to him a boy was curled up with his knees to his chest while shivering in fear.

The reason I screamed so loud was because, I can't find my items! Not one of them. My inventory is EMPTY!

"This has to be a bad joke. All my beloved items, I could cry!"

Damn it.

"At least that princess is probably coming faster now..." I looked at the cold wet stone floor and decided I am just gonna stand until that princess arrives.

"And what the hell are these? Since when did I have shackles on?" Looking at my wrists again I noticed massive shackles which also were on my legs.

"Ha, I didn't even notice that I broke them. But they're kinda cool so I will let them be."

What could I do now? Hmmm...

Aha! I could try some magic.

"Let's see."

Lifting my right hand again I concentrate and soon something began to form on my palm.

At first it was only as big as a pebble but it grew bigger and bigger and then it was the size of a billiard ball.

It is a little moon!

"Yess!"

That's moon magic. It's kinda like buff magic for werewolves like me. Even though my mana is pitifully low, most of them are skills and not magic directly.

silent crying noises

"Huh? Who's crying in here? Probably that guard hehe."

I closed my eyes for a moment and opened again.

The one who's crying is in the cell next to me.

Walking toward the wall that's separating him and me I knock on it.

"Knock knock."

Crack

"Waaah!" He screamed.

"oops." I swear I only knocked lightly!

As long as the wall doesn't crumble it's ok.

"Hellooo, I know you're there I can hear you silently crying like a baby kekeke."

"..." The crying stopped.

"Even if you stop crying now I already know you're there so don't be shy!" Oh man these people...

"... What do you want?" He said. He sounds young, like me. But I am on the manly young side while he's on the little kid young side.

"So you can talk, nice."

"..."

"..."

"and?"

"Oh, ah right I wanted to ask some questions." I said.

"why me? ..."

"Because you were the only one crying?"

"..."

"*sigh*, ok look, I woke up a few minutes ago and I don't know where I am and why I am here. So, could you tell me? Pretty please?"

I asked him so nicely he can't deny me!

"w-we are inside a prison." He said.

"No shit sherlock."

"Under the castle." He said. What a idiot.

"Go on, which kingdom dumbass." I knocked on the wall again.

"Hii! T-the Jioral Kingdom?"

"Huh? What the hell?" I've never heard of that Kingdom being in the new world before. Oh no. Does that mean...

"Hey, stupid kid." I said.

"W-what?" He sounded a tiny bit angry.

"Have you ever heard of the Baharuth Empire? Or the Re-Estize Kingdom? Or the Slane Theocracy?" I asked him hopefully.

"... No, I h-have never heard o-of them before.."

'Nononononononooooo! This can't be!' I thought.

"Fucking Shit, DAMNIT WHYYYY!!?" I roared.

Why the hell am I in the wrong world? Am I alone here?

"Yo kid!" I shouted.

"wa-what?" He answered.

step, step

"Oh never mind, I will ask you later again, seems like we got guests." And it's a small woman if the light steps are anything to go by.

The steps suddenly stopped as she seemed to halt in front of the kids cell

"Oh my, are you feeling better healer-san?" A feminine voice asked and I could tell instantly that she didn't give a shit how that kid felt.

She called him healer-san... Oh no.

"But today I am not here for you..."

step

"I came for you."

There she is. Flare. She is looking at me with this ugly grin she has.

She is one of the two bitch princesses from redo of healer. That means, the kid in the next cell is probably Keyaru. That crazy bastard.

"You know, it's really strange. One day you just fell from the sky and landed in the garden of the royal castle. But the thing is, you fell from very very veeery high, yet, not a scratch remains. What are you?" She said.

What a bitch. I don't like her one bit.

"I am the strongest Lycanthrope there is, bitch." It's the truth. In Yggdrasil, no one could be a challenge to me in a one by one, except Alduin and Ulkan. Even if three level hundred players teamed up on me I could defeat them most of the time. It really depends on what classes they have and if they have good equipment though.

"Lycan? Hmmm, I knew you mutated dogs had abnormal physical capabilities but not to this extend... And seems like the shackles made of magic strengthened steel did little to restrict you. Interesting." She said while looking me up and down.

"Shut the hell up, just tell me what you want, bitch." If I am honest I already made up a plan.

And it's pretty fucked up.

"I don't like your attitude, but don't worry, after a week with our esteemed heros I want to hear you calling me bitch again you filthy dog." She said with that crazy smile on her face.

"Why wait a week? Bitch. Now you don't have to wait." I said.

"Just you wait, I will get what I want." And after saying that she walked away.

I swear to god if that gay bastard with the canon even says something gay to me I will burn down this whole kingdom.

And that Blade hero can try me, we will see who will get fucked at the end.

"Okay, but before that, oy Keyaru!" Even though he's crazy, he's still a funny guy to be around.

"w-what?" he said.

"Want to be friends?"

Chapter 22: Let's get started for real now (Rewritten)

Since I got here a day ago I didn't even have the time to enjoy being in my favorite anime with overpowered abilities.

"Let's change that." Determined to live a fulfilling life I walk out of my giant chambers and make my way to the throne hall.

'Ahh, if I remember correctly today that village will be attacked. What was the name of it again? Can't remember." I thought while continuing on my way to the throne hall.

Ah, I forgot to mention Naberal and Lupus following me from behind. Damn they look so hot. That seducing smile of Lupus and the icy cold look in Naberals eyes are making me feel excited.

"So... How was your day?" Damn I am bad at initiating conversations.

However, they responded instantly.

"Every day in your glorious presence is a wonderful day m'lord!" Lupus said with a bright smile and a small hop in her step.

'Too cute. Ah, I am kinda glad the others aren't here now. Imagine us having a crush on the same girl, or girls. That would be nerve-wracking.' I thought.

"It is the utmost honor to serve you Lord Alduin and every day in your presence fulfills me with the greatest joy." She said respectfully.

"Oh, that's great." And after that it was silent all the way.

After a while we finally reached the thronw hall where Sebas was already waiting for me while bowing to me. He's such a good butler...

"Sebas, tell me where is Albedo?" I asked him.

"Should I call for her?" He said.

"No... I don't need her now... But tell me why they are taking so long to prepare Nazarick for a possible attack by enemies? A whole day to prepare is to much." I said. Sariel visibly felt very nervous.

'Oh man I shouldn't have said that so direct. I am always making them feel bad.' I thought seeing him like that and all the judging gazes from the others on him makes me feel like I am bullying him.

"I am deeply sorry my lord, I will tell them to hasten immediately, if you don't need me now of course." He said.

"No, you can go. But don't be too hard to them." I told him.

And with that he ran off.

"Anyway, let's see what we got here." I said as I sat down on my throne and looked at the cristal ball in my right hand.

On it I could see a big forest and going further I could make out some wood houses.

Thats it.

"Ohhh shit, it already started? I have to go. But before that..." I stood up and used the message spell.

'Albedo, meet me in the throne hall immediately. Fully amoured. We are going on a date.' Perfect.

Now I only have to wait a bi-

swoosh

"I AM HERE AND READY TO GO MY LORD!" An fully amored Albedo with bright glowing eyes and misty, warm and hectic breathing said while standing in front of me. Her mace tightly clenched in her hands.

'How did she even get the amor on so fast? But holy hell this isn't important now. I can smell great horny in her right now. It's dangerous.' I thought to myself while trying to keep calm.

"L-let me get amored first." I said.

"OF COURSE MY LORD!" Woah calm down.

With an unnecessary snap of my fingers I was now fully amored in my Black-golden armor that covered my whole body in heavy metal and my Slayer-Greatsword on my back.

"Ready to go I would say. You two stay here, we won't be gone for too long." I said to Naberal and Lupus who bowed to me in understanding.

"Greater Gate." I chanted while streching my hand out in front of me.

A big golden portal opened in front of us and Albedo and I stepped inside.

Chapter 23: 23. Village (Rewritten)

I felt so helpless. So weak. Never have I hated myself so much.

Mother and Father both died to these monsters. Only my little sister Nemu and I managed to flee into the woods but only because Father sacrificed himself to get us some time.

Only me and Nemu. Yes that's right, Nemu. She's still with me. I will protect her. I will keep her safe.

"Stop!" A big soldier said.

"Nemu!"

'NononononononNOOOO!!!' Why?! What should I do? These two followed us? What should I do?!

"Heheheee, look what we have here~" One of them said.

"She looks cute, doesn't she? What about we have some fun with her before we kill them?" The other said while stepping closer.

"Stop! Don't come closer!" I warned them, but as I expected, they didn't care and made fun of me.

"Sister *sob* I am scared. I want to Father and Mother. Uwaaa!" Nemu started crying.

It was like my heart got stabbed by a knife. The tears I tried to hold back the entire time started to fall.

I am scared too.

"Hey, why don't you take her and I will take the other one?" The first said.

"But she's a child... Argh, do what you want, just go somewhere I don't see you with her!" The other said.

What?

T-they want to t-take Nemu?

"Gahahahaaa! Don't worry! Now come on let's be fast before we have to return!"

Nononononononono.

"NO! Stay back!" I sbouted but they came closer anyway while we stepped back slowly. We can't run, Nemus leg is hurt and I am to tired to carry her!

But...

At least Nemu has to be saved.

"Y-you can take me... I won't resist, but please, I beg of you *sob* let my sister go! Please!" I said falling on my knees before them. Crying.

I feel so weak.

But then he spoke.

It was so slow that every word echoed through my head.

"Why. Should. We?" He said and jumped on me.

"NEMU RUN!" I stood up and ran at him, trying to tackle him but he just punched me and Nemu stood frozen in fear.

I failed. Why does this have to happen to us? Why aren't the soldiers of our kingdom coming to safe us?

Where is the strong warrior I need?

"GAHAHAHA-wha-! *crunch*" He was laughing loud but then something happened.

A golden gate of some sort opened and something came out of it and just stomped on the man which completly crushed his chest, even with armor on.

It was a shocking sight.

It had a full body armor with golden accent and a giant slab of metal on his back that resembles a sword but is way to big to be one.

This wasn't something, it was SOMEONE. He was, so big, so strong.

"So beautiful."

"You ok?" Is what he spoke to me. Such magnificent words...

-Alduin POV:

After stepping trough the portal I arrived just before something cruel happened.

Suprisingly there was a soldier on the other side laughing like a madman so I just stomped on him which completly crushed him.

Talk about cool entrance.

Turning around I saw Enri laying on the ground with a tear stained face.

"So beautiful." She said as she saw me.

Well thanks I guess. I sure look badass in the armor.

"You ok?" I asked her as I walked closer to her. Wow normal humans sure are small. But well I am easily 2.30 meters with the armor on.

"I-I'm, please help us. Our village, is getting attacked." She slowly said while staring at me.

"Hmm, let's get you and your sister healed up and-" As I was aboit to propose something I was interrupted by a voice.

"WH-WHO ARE YOU?!" Shouted the soldier whom I forgot he was there. He was shacking all over and pointing his pathetic sword at me.

The blood and flesh remains all over my right leg probably makes me look more menacing.

"You dare to interrupt my Lord?!" Albedo said aggressively but I told her to stay put with a signal from my hand which she understood and obeyed.

"Let's try something on you." I said as I stretched my hand out pointing at him.

"What a-are you doing?!" The soldier became scared and backed off.

"Grasp Heart." I said.

Slowly a heart started forming in my hand. It was still pulsating and looked very alive.

"S-stop it!" He screamed and rushed at me but before he could move any closer I crushed the Heart in my palm which made him fall forward like a puppet whose strings had been cut.

'Yeah I understand why it's Momongas favourite spell. Effective and cool as hell.' I thought to myself.

"Anyway, here drink this and wait here, I will see what I can do for your village." I said to Enri while giving a side glance to Nemu. The poor girl has been crying all the time.

Walking over to her I gave her a had pat, but very, very carefully of course, don't want to crush her head. That would be gruesome.

"Everything is gonna be alright, look after you big sister for me will you?" I said to her.

"*sob* Thank you, I will *sob*" She said, seems like she calmed down a bit.

Taking a last glance at her I went to the village.

'Man, Nemu really reminds me of that little brat. Oh no, don't cry Alduin, don't cry.' I don't want to regret coming here! But I already miss Hinata and that brat.

Sigh

"My Love-uh My Lord I mean, what is it that makes you sigh like that?" Albedo asked me with concern in her voice.

That made me smile a little.

"Nothing to worry about, I just remembered something unpleasant. Let us hurry so we can have a real date afterwards." I said with a smile which couldn't be noticed because the helmet I wear.

"As you command!" She said and ran off.

I, of course, catched up with her easily and after a few seconds of running in her speed we arrived at the Village.

The stench of burned wood and blood assaulted my nose. The screams of dying villagers still echoed around.

"Assemble them all here!" The captain ordered.

And the soldiers heeding his command assembled all the remaining villagers in front of the captain.

Meanwhile Albedo and me were walking towards them calmly. And probably because of the pressure I naturally gave off I left a trail of my footsteps. The dirt I stepped on even slightly turned black.

"Huh? Who are you and what is your business here?! No, you know what, just get him and kill him too!" The captain ordered as he saw the two of us approaching.

But since we don't care we kept walking towards him ignoring the horde of soldiers storming at us.

Suddenly a probably higher ranking soldier whispered something in the captains ear.

And I could hear it too of course.

'How amusing, heh.' I thought.

"Soldiers! Kill that big Black-gold guy but leave the woman alone, just capture her!" He odered with a smirk.

Hearing what their captain told them the soldiers snickered.

But suddenly the ground began to shake.

"You ants! You pathetic, worthless fools! You dare to talk like that in presence of the Lord himself?! You shall pay dearly for it!" Albedo went full worship-yandere mode and started to rip the soldiers near us apart. But with a quick message I told her to not show anything over the top in terms of power which she of course obeyed. Of course I don't care about the soldiers seeing our power since they die anyway, but I still want to keep the villagers alive and sane.

~

"W-what are you?! Why are you doing this?!" The captain stepped back in fear.

Albedo already finished ripping the soldiers apart and seems to have enjoyed it alot.

Honestly I wanted to fight some too but well, there is an army waiting for me later anyway.

I would kill that captain guy too but I need some information, or want some information better said. Not need.

And the first thing that came to my mind was to send that rude guy to Neuronist Painkill.

"You. Come to me and you will live, but if you run away now..." I pointed at him and said that. I just don't want to run around, that wouldn't look so elegant.

"Y-you, how can I trust you? You will kill me anyway!" He said, and ran away...

"Little Shit." I said but then remembered something.

"My Lord, shall I?" Albedo asked respectfully.

"No need." I answered.

I just remembered an usesless spell that's gonna be overpowered combined with my strength.

And that's Telekinesis.

Stretching my hand out to the running man I activated the spell that now slowly sapped away at my enormous mana reserves. I would guess I could use this spell for a week or two straight until my mana is depleted, or maybe even three weeks.

Anyway, the strength of my Telekinesis is as strong as I am physically capable. So it's almost useless for mages, but unnecessary high mana usage for warriors and the likes.

But if you are something like me...

It could crush mountains.

"WHAT IS HAPPENING?! STOP! STOP IT!" The captain who started floating and wiggling in the air shouted.

"No, I told you." I said.

"GUGH!"

I put a little strength in my grip. Outwards I may look like a cold statue but right now I was excited.

'That's so damn cool! Man I feel strong star wars vibes with this one hehe.' I thought.

"Gate. And here you go." I said as I opened a gate to Neuronist Painkill's little room and threw him in.

"Painkill, I want as much information as possible!" I said and tried to hastily close the gate but it was too late.

"KYAAA! LLLORD ALDUIN?! ARE-ARE YOU VISI-" A green woman made out of slime squealed. She was naked. But had a body putting even Albedo to shame. Her huge boobs were jiggling and she was running at the gate. Yes. That is Neuronist Painkill.

"Holy shit, he created a monster. That crazy bastard." I said as I closed the gate fast.

"Tch. Whore." Albedo silently spat.

Shoermel that dog thought it would be a good idea to give her a "true" form and shape-shifting ability. Now she looks like a cute slime milf you would find only in the best colored hentais.

Now that's a good thing, I agree. Buuut..

She still has that ugly ass form she uses to torture her victims.

shiver

'In the anime it was already bad, that form, but in real it's ten times worse. At least she changes to that sexy form instantly when she sees me. But she gets crazy every time she sees me.' I thought to myself. Shalltear would be the same case but I made her true Vampire form, how do I say this, less ugly and more elegant?

Anyway.

"Where is the village chief? I need to talk to him about my payment." I said to the villagers that, even though they were relieved the soldiers are dead, are still scared shitless because of Albedo. Honestly, I understand that.

"S-sir knight. Ehem I a-apologize, I mean Lord?" An eldery man stood up and talked.

"Hmm, you can call me... ehm... Call me... Al." I said.

'Ah damnit! Where are the cool names when you need them?! *sigh* And Al? What was I thinking? Too late now anyway...' I thought while Albedo looked at me strangely.

'Why would Lord Alduin do that? It has to be part of his big plan Demiurge told me about! Ahhh~ the lord truly is the greatest mind to ever exist.' Is what Albedo thought.

"T-then, Lord Al? Shall we talk about the payment now? Please follow me." He said respectfully.

"Ah, I found two girls in that forest before I came here, send someone to get them here." I ordered him.

"O-of course! You two, can you two go please? Thank you. Now follow me please Lord Al." After he told two of the assembled villagers to fetch Enri and Nemu we finally got to talk about the payment.

I of course only wanted the information they may have not shown in the Anime and then get their endless gratitude for killing that whole army. Apparently the Slane Theocracy got a new saint or something like that he told me. That definitely wasn't in the Anime. Probably unimportant for now.

Ah, and I want to have Gazef Stronoff. For me it kinda sucked that Momonga just let him stay dead like that after killing him.

I want him to serve me with utmost loyalty like he does with his current king.

But now I only need to gain his favour.

"Ah, and here they come. Old man, follow me outside but tell everyone else to hide. We have guests." And with that I walked outside with Albedo of course following me.

The Old man looked stressed out, probably thinking they were being attacked again but did as I told him.

~

Now standing outside I was waiting for them to arrive as I already saw them approaching.

The Village chief was sweating buckets and shivering too.

"They're from the Re-Estiz Kingdom and not our enemies." I told him.

"*sigh* I am glad. But Lord Al, if I may ask, how could you tell?" He asked me with uncertainty in his eyes.

"Good eyes." I answer shortly.

As the small team of mercenary looking soldiers arrived they stopped their horses som distance away from us and a big buffed man with a beard walked towards me.

'Nice muscles, but mine are bigger and stronger! Hehe' I thought with a smirk.

Gazef looked at me with sharp eyes and analysed everything in the short time he had while walking to me. As he saw the gigantic sword on my back his eyes narrowed even further then they already were.

To be honest, I would be cautious too. Currently I am standing in front of a half burned down Village with bloodstains all around and not a single person except corpses everywhere on the ground. Plus the fact that I am very tall and broad too with this kind of sword on my back.

I would rate myself dark souls-hardest-boss-in-the-game level.

"Greetings, my name is Gazef Stronoff and I wad sent by the king because of the enemy attacks all around the borderland. I assume they attack this village too?" He spoke in a grave tone.

"Indeed they have attacked this Village but as I was passing by I thought I would help out, for payment of course." I answered him to which the village chief nodded confirming my words.

As expected, Gazef went down on his knee and thanked me for saving the town bla bla bla.

"Friend, would you tell me your name?" He asked with a smile.

'Friend? Sure why not.' I thought, but before I could answer Albedo did.

"Be honored to be in his presence and fall on your knees maggot for your are standing before the allmighty lord-"

Bonk

"Call me Al." I said to him after bonking Albedos head which she was now comically holding while sitting on the ground. Too cute.

"HAHAHA! What a woman you have Al! Oh, I should call you Lord Al shouldn't I? Where are you from and why are you wandering these lands if I may ask Lord Al? You sure look strong." He asked curiously.

Damn he talks way more than shown in the Anime. But from that I can guess he already trusts me more than he did Momonga at this point.

"I rather not talk about that, bad memories if you know what I mean." I said to him with thw saddest voice I could.

"Hm, I understand. I am sorry for bringing up bad memories my friend. Hm? What is it?" He apologized but then one of the soldiers who just came back for scouting gave him the news of the army surounding them and his face got serious in a split second.

"Seems like they really want you." I said.

"I have to go... But before that, can I ask you of a favour? Would you help me with this fight, I would pay you-" He wanted to ask for help but I did exactly what Momonga did and denied but instead promised to keep the villagers safe. He thanked me and before he left I gave him that place switch item which name I forgot.

~

Chapter 25: 25. Devasted (Rewritten)

Yo.

Just wanted to show you guys something a reader posted but deleted again.

Here.

~

"You fool really thought you could win against this many angels?! You are gonna die and after that we will raid that village you tried to protect with your life! GAHAHAH!" The bald commander of the enemy said.

How funny.

"Heheha... AHAHAHAHAAA!" I couldn't help but laugh.

"What?! Did you go crazy? Why are YOU laughing?!" He asked me aggressively.

"hahaha... You said you want to raid the village I am protecting? HAHAHAA! THERE IS A WARRIOR THERE, MANY TIMES STRONGER THAN MYSELF AND HIS COMPANION! I DIDN'T EVEN SEE HIM FIGHT AND ALREADY KNEW THAT I COULDN'T EVEN DREAM OF GETTING A SCRATCH ON HIM!!!" I told them. Lord Al will keep his promise. I know it.

And what I said is true. The moment I laid my eyes on him I already felt like giving up! He is a monster. A good one from what I've seen.

"You truly have gone mad Gazef! But don't worry, I will free you of your madness! Angels kill him!" The bald captain gave the final command.

'Ahhh, that's it then? I still had so much to do for the kingdom. And the king is already old and needs me too... At least I can die knowing I made friends with an individual such as Lord Al. Though, I would love to see him fight...' I thought with a sad smile on my face as the angels were approaching fast.

swish

They all at once stabbed me...

That's it then I guess....

...

"CAPTAIN?! Go get the village doctor! Captain what happened and how did you get here?!" Some old man questioned me.

Why am I screamed at by some old man the second I die? *sigh* wait... Pain, I still feel great pain! Am I still alive?

"Al... Where is Lord Al?" I asked weakly. The blood loss is too much, I am about to pass out.

"He... He just dissapeared! It's like he switched places with you captain!" The village chief said.

What? Switched places? Oh.. I get it now hahaha.

"That bastard hahahaaha..." And with that I passed out.

~

'Took him long enough to get beaten up. Anyway, now I can have some fun.' I thought as I appeared in front of some low-tier angels.

"What?! Where is Gazef? And who are you?!" Some bald dude whose name I forgot screamed at me.

"My name is Alduin, and I am the one who is protecting the village you talked about earlier. Now, accept defeat and maybe you will live for a while afterwards." I told them. Of course they won't give up and of course they will all die.

"YOU THINK YOU CAN DEMAND FROM ME?! ANGELS, KILL THAT BASTARD!" He definitely is short-fused.

On his command the angels started approaching me and Albedo was about to step in but I told her to stay where she is until I am done here. And after that we will finally have our date which hopefully gets a happy ending if you know what I mean.

So these Angels began their barrage of attacks... which did absolutely no damage at all... Which was exactly what I expected.

"WHAT THE HELL ARE YOU DOING?! KILL HIM, NOW!" The bald captain screamed nervously.

He probably remembered what Gazef told him before and slowly starts believing. As he should.

As I was seeing absolutely nothing because of the tens of angels attacking me from the front I used my telekinesis and just squashed them like some insects.

"Hahaha! You see now how helpless your situation is you pathetic bug?! Bow before the might of Lord Alduin and accept death!" Albedo shouted excited from the side lines while swinging her arms in the air.

She kinda reminds me of some highschool cheerleader...

This makes me wanna go all out.

"I-impossible! Nothing can beat me! No one!" Stage one, denial.

"Come on, just pull out that big angel. It's getting boring already." I said while waving my hand at him. Maybe I should just start killing them? But what should I use? Mass-destruction spells or just my physical capabilities? Ah! I will use Telekinesis combined with my sword to slaughter them all! That's it!

'Wow I can't wait too see how I will turn out once my karma stat starts kickin in.' I hope I don't become some emotionless dude. That would be sad.

"W-WHAT?! HOW DO YOU KNOW ABOUT THIS?! No, doesn't matter, DOMINION AUTHORITY! COME KILL THAT DEMON!" He screamed hysterically holding the summoning crystal up in the air with both of his arms.

summoning noises

As the big ass angel appeared in all his holy glory most of the small holy army fell on their knees and started praying. All while that bald guy was laughing...

"KILL HIMMMM!" He shouted for the tenth time.

"MwuahahahahahahaAHAHAHAHA! [Reality Slash]! Hehehehe!" I equipped my great sword, even if not needed, and used reality slash. A very strong 10th Tier spell that as it name says cuts realty itself. I could also just wave my hand to cast it but I like using my sword. Alone the swing of my greatsword sent a strong wind against the army.

And before the Dominion Authority could even move it was cleanly cut in half from head to toe and just exploded in particles.

And like that, hell broke loose among the soldiers.

"No, nonononoNOOOOO! THIS IS IMPOS-"

SLASH

Before I have to hear him crying around like that again I rather end this fast and have my date with dear Albedo.

And like that I just vanished in the eyes of the soldiers and in the next moment the head of their captain just flew into the air and exploded.

Speeding around I hacked down soldiers left and right which resulted in heavy shockwaves being created and causing the nearby soldiers and their limbs to fly around.

"Kyaaaa! Go My Lord! Show them your power!" Albedo squealed as hot misty breath escaped her helmet.

She truly is a good waifu. Cheering for me like that.

After about fifteen seconds later all that was left was a mountain of severed limbs and crushed bodies.

To be honest, I don't feel anything with killing them all. I expected some sort of disgust or reluctance but there's nothing like that.

Guess that's the dragon taking over and adding my True Neutral Karma stat it would make some sense I guess.

Anyway.

Now that I finished them it's time for some favourite girl action...

Oh, and no I did not forget about those guys spying on me. It's all going as planned Hahahahah!

"Come on Albedo! Let's go have a date." I said as I walked away and Albedo following me with a small happy jump in her steps.

~~~~~~~~~

Finally done wirh the rewrite, if any of you have ANY suggestions as small as they may be tell me before I finish my next chap and you will be heard.

Made in United States
Troutdale, OR
01/08/2025

27724021R00058